THE
ST PATRICK'S
TREASURY

THE
ST PATRICK'S
TREASURY

JOHN KILLEN

·THE·
BLACK
·STAFF·
PRESS

To Eoghan, Anna, Fionn,
Catherine and Peter

Published in 2018 by Blackstaff Press
an imprint of Colourpoint Creative Ltd, Colourpoint House,
Jubilee Business Park, 21 Jubilee Road,
Newtownards, BT23 4YH

The acknowledgements on pages 244–49
constitute an extension of this copyright page.

Printed in Antrim by W&G Baird Limited

A CIP catalogue for this book is available from the
British Library

ISBN 978-0-85640-958-5

www.blackstaffpress.com

CONTENTS

PREFACE

St Patrick is the patron saint of Ireland; he is acknowledged as the rugged follower of Christ who introduced Christianity to the pagan people of fifth-century Ireland. His renown is worldwide, and St Patrick's Day is now almost universally celebrated. Yet, Patrick was not the first Irish saint. Before he began his mission, Saints Declan, Ailbe, Ciaran, Abban and Ibar were ministering to their small Christian flocks in Leinster, Wexford, Limerick, Birr and Ardmore. The pre-eminence of Patrick as patron saint of Ireland arises mainly from two biographies of the saint – Muirchú's *Life of Saint Patrick* and Jocelin's *Life and Acts of Saint Patrick*. Both works are hagiographical, treating the saint as a wonder-worker capable of the most astounding feats of magic inspired by his closeness to God.

Muirchú's *Life* almost certainly arose from the challenge to the hegemony of the See of Armagh by the Munster churchmen in the seventh century. Aedh, Bishop of Sletty (on the border of Carlow and Laois), affiliated his church with Armagh's claims to metropolitan status and asked the monk, Muirchú, to write the *Life of Saint Patrick*. Muirchú's *Life* credited Patrick with the conversion of Ireland before the spread of monasticism, and stressed the pre-eminence of Patrick's church of Armagh. The *Life* was copied by the scribe, Ferdomnach, from the original into the *Book of Armagh* in 807, along with writings acknowledged to have been written by St Patrick: his *Confessio* and *Letter to Coroticus*.

Jocelin's work was commissioned by the Norman knight, John De Courcey, who is reputed by Phillips, the historian of Dundrum Castle in County Down, to have studied the 'majority of the sixty-two lives of St Patrick, which historians tell us were extant in his day … that he might, by the knowledge acquired, be enabled to take a firmer grip of the character, affections and habits of the Irish, over whom he meantime ruled as the first Earl of Ulster.'

Little is actually known about the historical figure, Patrick. Accounts of his miracles are legion; his connection with snakes and shamrock is retold on an almost daily basis, and his iconic image is instantly recognisable across the world. The dates of his birth and death are, however, contested by scholars, the date of his return to Ireland to begin his mission is problematic and the very nature of his mission has been questioned. The prominent Patrician scholar, Ludwig Bieler, aware of these issues, made a very simple and sensible suggestion in his 1948 publication, *The Life and Legend of Saint Patrick*: 'It is not the man that counts, however striking was his personality, but the faith that he brought …'

This anthology sets out to follow the footsteps of St Patrick, showing the enormous range of research and interest there has been in the saint in the sixteen centuries since he walked this land. These extracts seek to explore what Patrick meant to people through the centuries, and what he now may mean to people in the twenty-first century. Included are interpretations of his mission, the poetry and art he inspired and the modern historiography of academic scholars. The writings of Patrick are reproduced as key sources for our understanding of the saint; Patrician relics and representations are examined; as are the traditions, myths and legends that surround him. Finally, the Loci Patricii – those places not just in Ireland but across the world which have been intimately associated with the saint and his cult – are addressed, showing his universal appeal.

In the Patrician year, 1961, the then Roman Catholic Bishop of Clonfert, William Philbin (who wrote in Irish as Liam Mac Philibin), wrote a biography of St Patrick in the Irish language. In his introduction he described Patrick's importance to Ireland:

There is no greater name in Irish history than Patrick son of Calpruinn … He was the author of the greatest and most influential change ever to come to our race bringing them the grace of belief in God …

His Protestant counterpart, George Otto Simms, Archbishop of Armagh and Primate of All Ireland (1969–80), wrote in 1988:

We rejoice on St. Patrick's day, that the saint, who had spent his youth in Ireland as a slave, came back with a spirit of reconciliation and a deep love for the people of this island. A voice called him back; vast numbers were to find new life, and a Christian hope through this pilgrim who journeyed among them…

These two important twentieth century Irish religious authors, one Catholic and one Protestant, are symbolic of Patrick's role in the Irish psyche. Implicit in their contributions is the history of Patrick and his place in Irish life over sixteen hundred years. Underlying their words, key moments in Irish history can be understood: the primacy of Armagh as put forward by Muirchú; the development of the Irish church under Norman rule in Ireland in the twelfth and thirteenth centuries through Jocelin's writings; the Reformation in Ireland in the sixteenth and seventeenth centuries and its effects on the people of Ireland; the sectarianism of the nineteenth and twentieth centuries and the very partial reconciliation of a divided people in the early part of the twenty-first. In toto, these extracts help explain the making of Patrick, patron saint of Ireland.

1

THE LIFE OF ST PATRICK

B ecause we are so familiar with the name St Patrick, and so familiar with the celebration of St Patrick's Day each year on 17th March, we can be shocked and a little distressed at how little we actually know about the man himself. But when we realise the dearth of fifth-century sources for history – any history – we begin to appreciate the challenge of St Patrick.

Biography we understand; hagiography is a leap of faith – but all religion is faith based. The facts of St Patrick's life are few, and all subsequent works on the life of Ireland's patron saint necessarily follow Muirchú's *Life of Saint Patrick* as it appeared in the ninth-century *Book of Armagh*. Each subsequent generation of biographer or hagiographer wrote for the people of his or her time, enhancing or embellishing the story.

This has allowed for the wide variety of treatment of the *Life of Saint Patrick* by different, and differing, authors. The saint's chronology has often been argued over, and radically different dates and places of birth given: author John Armstrong, writing in 1859, stated that Patrick was born in 'AD 387 at Taberna, near Dumbarton' in Scotland; while in 2013, another author, Marcus Losack, stated equally authoritatively that in 'AD 385 Patrick is born in Brittany (possibly at Tours – *Nemthor/Naem-Tour* – or on the family estate at Bannavem Tiburniae).'

His life has been simplified for children to understand; and addressed with the rigour of scholarly research for academics to contest. The Annals of Ulster, the Annals of Innisfallen and the Annals of Ireland are used to attempt to pin down the years of his birth, life and ministry in Ireland. The Latin of his *Confessio* and *Letter to Coroticus* is analysed and translated to better understand his education in preparation for, and the work of, his mission: but precision eludes us. All propositions concerning the facts of his life are now prefaced with words such as *probably*, *presumably*, *arguably* etc.

But this is in the nature of patron saints. Despite the most rigorous academic studies of the social, religious and political nature of fifth-century Ireland, Britain, Europe and the world, we retain our basic understanding of St Patrick, patron saint of Ireland. This includes his conversion of the Irish to Christianity, his banishing of the snakes, his use of the shamrock to explain the Trinity, and his death on 17 March.

Two lines from two different authors sum up the essence of the man. One is, 'Patrick is the most important figure in Irish Christian history.' (Cormac Bourke, 2009) The other is, 'There is no greater name in Irish history than Patrick, son of Calpruinn.' (William Philbin, 1961).

Diocese of Down and Connor

'Patrick consecrated by Pope Celestine',
St Patrick's Church, Saul

Mise Pádraig

Níl ainm ar bith i stair na hÉireann is mó ná Pádraig Mac Calpruinn. Níor mhair aoinne sa tír seo riamh ba mhó le rá ag clanna Gael ná aoinne ab fhearr a thuill a ghradam. B'é b'údar leis an athrú ba thábhachtaí agus ba thairbhí dá dtáinig riamh ar shaol ár gcine; agus, ag altú grásta an chreidimh do Dhia dóibh abhus agus i gcéin, níorbh fhaillí le Gaeil am ar bith a mbuíochas a ghabháil le hAspal na hÉireann. Bíodh a fhianaise sin ar na céadta eaglais ar fud an domhain a bhfuil Pádraig mar phátrún acu (deirtear gur líonmhaire iad ná a bhfuil coisricthe do naomh ar bith eile cé is moite den Mhaighdin Bheannaithe), ar an méid daoine a mbaistear a ainm orthu, agus ar cheiliúradh a fhéile, sa mbaile agus I gcéin, mar fhéile náisiúnta na hEireann.

There is no greater name in Irish history than Patrick, son of Calpruinn. No one ever lived in this country who was more highly regarded among the peoples of Ireland nor who more deserved the honour. He was the author of the greatest and most influential change to ever come on our race, bringing the people the grace of belief in God both far and wide. From then on people have constantly praised the Apostle of Ireland. This is evident in the number of churches throughout the world which have Patrick as their patron (it is said to be greater than any other apart from the Blessed Virgin), the number of people who have been given his name and the fact that his feast day is celebrated both at home and abroad as the national feast day in Ireland.

Liam Mac Philibin
Mise Pádraig, 1961
Translated by Mary Delargy

We Rejoice on St. Patrick's Day

We rejoice on St. Patrick's day, that the saint, who had spent his youth in Ireland as a slave, came back with a spirit of reconciliation and a deep love for the people of this island. A voice called him back; vast numbers were to find new life and a Christian hope through this pilgrim who journeyed among them; this prophet who had a word which triumphed over evil; this personality who was both hated and loved, whose life was marked by both failure and faith, whose attachment to Ireland with 'its whirling winds, and tempests; its glorious sunshine and pale white moonlight', was wholehearted. The beauty and the struggle of life shone through his story of voices and visions, as well as in his dark moments and much else that thwarted him.

George Otto Simms
Angels and Saints, 1988

Patrick of Ireland

Much of Patrick's life is shrouded in mystery and historians differ on the probable chronology of the saint's life. Fortunately, he has left behind two documents, his *Confession* and his *Letter to Coroticus,* which describe some of his experiences. He was not the first Christian missionary to reach Ireland, but the principal credit for converting the pagan island and establishing the Celtic Church belongs to him.

He was the son of a Roman official, Calpurnius, living probably in Wales. As a boy of sixteen, Patrick was captured by raiders and sold to an Irish chieftain, Milchu. He spent years in slavery, herding sheep on Slemish Mountain in Co. Antrim. He escaped following a dream in which a voice told him a ship would be waiting to take him to his own country. After a journey of 200 miles he found the ship, and was eventually able to return to his family.

One night, in a dream, he heard voices calling him back to Ireland. It is thought that he studied under Saint Germanus at Auxerre, France, and that his mission to Ireland was approved due to the early death of Saint Palladius, who had been sent as a bishop to the Irish 'believing in Christ' in 431. Consequently, 432 is the traditional date for Patrick's voyage to Ireland, which ended on the shores of Strangford Lough. He quickly made a convert of a local chief named Dichu, who gave him a barn at Saul, Co. Down, for his first church.

Before long Patrick made his way to the Hill of Tara, Co. Meath, seat of the high king of Ireland. Arriving on the eve of Easter, he lit paschal fire on the nearby Hill of Slane. At this time of year, it was pagan practice to put out all fires before a new one was lit at Tara. When the druids at Tara saw the light from Slane, they warned King Laoghaire that he must extinguish it or it would burn forever. Patrick was summoned to Tara, and on the way he and his followers chanted the hymn known as 'The Lorica' or 'Saint Patrick's Breastplate'. Although Laoghaire remained a pagan, he was so impressed by the saint that he gave him permission to make converts throughout his realm. Muirchu's *Life of Patrick*, written two centuries later, describes a contest of magic in which Laoghaire's druids had to concede victory to the saint.

Patrick travelled widely in Ireland, making converts and establishing new churches, though he eventually made his headquarters at Armagh. On one occasion he spent the forty days of Lent on a mountain in Co. Mayo which is now called Croagh Patrick. He was harassed by demons in the form of blackbirds, clustered so densely that the sky was black, but he continued to pray, and rang his bell to disperse assailants.

An angel then appeared to tell the saint that all his petitions for the Irish people would be granted, and that they would retain their Christian faith until Judgement Day. There are many legends about Patrick, not least that he banished snakes from Ireland and that he adopted the shamrock as a symbol of the Holy Trinity.

Patrick's writings belong to the latter part of his life and confirm that he was less learned as a writer than he was persuasive as a speaker. Nonetheless, the *Confession*, a response to criticisms of his mission in Ireland, is a moving revelation of his vocation and of the divine guidance he received in dreams. Irish annals give the date of Patrick's death as 493, but an earlier date of 461 seems more likely. Tradition says he died at Saul and was buried at nearby Downpatrick.

Martin Wallace
Saints of the Celtic Church, 2008

Saint Patrick

When darkness lay across the land
Saint Patrick lit the Paschal flame
And kindled in the hearts of men
A veneration for the name
Of God, and Jesus Christ His Son,
Who freely gave His life away
And by the shedding of His blood
Redeemed all men at Calvary.
And so they turned from ancient ways,
The pagan gods, the wicked strife,
To hear the creed of gentleness
The promise of eternal life,
And 'ere Saint Patrick's task was done
His converts travelled far and wide

Until the Christian bell was heard
To sound in every countryside.

John Irvine
A Treasury of Irish Saints, 1964

Calendar of the Saints: Patrick

Seaghán Mac Cathmhaoil

JANUARY
Patric was born about the year 373 A.D. in France or Scotland.
When the babe was born, no water was to be found for baptism,
so the priest, who was blind, took the infant's hand in his, and
with it blessed the ground, and there burst up on the spot a well
of clear spring water, in which the child was baptised.

FEBRUARY
When Patric came to be a boy, pirates came to his native land,
and after killing many of his people, they took Patric and his
sister to Ireland, where they were sold as slaves.

MARCH

There was a rich man named Milcho, who lived at that time near the mountain of Slieve Mish, in the north. He bought Patric and put him to herd his swine on the mountain. After some time the boy fled from Milcho, and sailed across the seas to his own country.

APRIL

After many years of study Patric was consecrated Bishop and returned to Ireland about the year 432 A.D. as missioner. After a long voyage, his ship came to land at Wicklow, but he had to depart from this place, for the chief of the country refused him leave to remain in it.

MAY

Patric sailed north till he came to Lough Cuan. There he landed, but Dicho, the chief of that district let loose his two great hounds. Patric raised his cross, and the hounds whimpered and fawned on the holy man. Dicho was seized with anger and drew his sword, but he lost the power of his limbs. The chief became afraid, believed in Patric and was baptised.

JUNE

Patric had a mind to solemnise the Easter Fire at Tara, and so he journeyed to Moy Breagh, and there he lit the Paschal Fire. The Ard Righ saw it, and he was very angry, for the people were forbidden, during the great Pagan Festival, to light their fires before the great Druidical Fire at Tara. So Laoghaire sent his messenger to Patric and ordered him to come before him.

JULY

Patric, with the boy Benignus, came to Tara, and a great discussion then arose between the Saint and Luchru, the Druid. 'Let us have a contest,' said Luchru, 'till it be seen which of us has the greater power. I am so powerful that I can raise myself to the sky.' He raised himself to the sky, but Patric called on God, and the Druid fell to the ground and was killed. Patric then preached a great sermon, and after many manifestations of his power, the King and his warriors were seized with terror and threw themselves at the feet of Patric and were baptised.

Seaghán Mac Cathmhaoil

AUGUST

When Patric was explaining to the multitudes the mystery of the Trinity, he saw that they did not understand. He lowered his head in thought, and saw at his feet a dewy shamrock. He pulled it and showed it to the people. 'Look,' he said, 'this little plant has but one stem, yet it has three leaves, equal in every respect. In like manner, there is but one God, but in him there are three Persons, distinguishable and equal in all things.' The people then understood better the nature of the Trinity, and believed.

SEPTEMBER

Eaoghaire had two daughters, Ethnea and Fedelm, and as was their custom they went to the well, called Clebach, to bathe; as they approached they were astonished to see Patric and his clerics praying there. 'Who are ye, and whence come ye?' asked Ethnea, and Patric answered, ''Twere better for you to confess the true God than to be enquiring whence we come.' The Saint then told the maidens of God and the wonders of heaven. They believed, and were baptised, and died.

Seaghán Mac Cathmhaoil

OCTOBER

Patric journeyed to Cashel of the Kings, and it is said that on his approach, the images of the false gods fell to the ground. He preached to the people, and King Angus was baptised. It is said that the Saint, when putting his crozier in the earth, drove it through the foot of his King, not knowing it. Patric seeing the earth red with blood, asked Angus why he did not complain, and he answered that he thought it was part of the baptism. Patric wondered, and blessed the King.

NOVEMBER

Patric was now an old man and came to die, and Brigid journeyed from Kildare with his winding sheet. The Saint came to know that she was faint and could not finish her journey, so he sent his horses and chariots to bring Brigid and her company to Saul.

Seaghán Mac Cathmhaoil

DECEMBER

About the year 493 A.D. Patric's soul left his body, while Brigid and Etembria and the monks of Saul stood around him. He was buried after twelve days in Down, and it is said that a bright light shone over the monastery during that time.

Seaghán Mac Cathmhaoil
Calendar of the Saints, 1907

Hymnus in Laudem Sancti Patricii

Audite
Hear, all ye who love God, the holy merits
of Patrick the bishop, a man blessed in Christ:
how, for his good deeds, he is likened unto the angels,
and, for his perfect life, is comparable to the apostles.

Beata
In all things he keepeth Christ's blessed commandments;
his works shine forth brightly among men:
and these follow his holy, wonderful example;
whence, also, they magnify the Lord, the Father in heaven.

Constans
Steadfast in the fear of God, and in faith immovable,
upon him, as upon Peter, the Church is built:
and he hath been allotted his apostleship by God;
against him the gates of hell prevail not.

Dominus
The Lord chose him to teach the barbarous
nations, and to fish with the nets of doctrine:
and from the world to draw believers unto grace,
who should follow the Lord to the ethereal abode.

Electa
He tradeth with Christ's choice Gospel-talents,
which among the Irish tribes he doth require with interest:
hereafter, as reward for the pains of this labour of voyaging,
he shall possess the joy of the heavenly kingdom with Christ.

Fidelis
The faithful servant and eminent messenger of God,
he sheweth good men an apostolic example and pattern:
to God's folk he preacheth by acts as well as by words,
that he may stir up by good deeds the man whom he
    converteth not by speech.

Gloriam
With Christ he hath glory, in the world honour;
he is venerated by all as an angel of God:
him hath God sent, like Paul, as an apostle to the Gentiles,
that he might lead the way for men unto the Kingdom of God.

Humilis
Humble in spirit and body through the fear of God,

upon him, for his good deeds, the Lord resteth:
in his righteous flesh he beareth the *stigmata* of Christ;
and in his cross alone doth glory, staying himself thereon.

Impiger

Unwearied, he feedeth believers with celestial repasts,
lest those who are seen in Christ's company should faint by the way:
to these he distributeth, as loaves, Gospel-words;
and in his hands they are multipled, as was the manna.

Kastam

For the love of the Lord he keepeth chaste his flesh;
which flesh he hath prepared as a temple for the Holy Spirit:
by whom, in pure activities, it is continually possessed;
and he doth offer it to God as a living and acceptable sacrifice.

Lumenque

And he is the great, burning Gospel-light of the world (*mundi*);
raised upon a candlestick, shining through the whole world
(*sæculo*):
the King's fortified city, set on a hill;
wherein is much store which the Lord doth possess.

Maximus

For greatest in the kingdom of heaven shall he be called
who fulfilleth in good actions what by sacred words he teacheth:
he excelleth as a good example and pattern to the faithful;
and in a pure heart he hath confidence toward God.

Nomen

He proclaimeth boldly to the tribes the Name of the Lord,
to whom he giveth the eternal grace of the laver of salvation:
for their offences he prayeth daily unto God;

for them also he offers up to the God worthy sacrifices *(dignas immolat hostias)*

Omnem
All the glory of the world he spurneth for the law divine;
all things, compared with His [God's] table he counteth as chaff:
nor is he moved by the violent thunderbolt of this world,
but rejoiceth in afflictions when he doth suffer for Christ.

Pastor
The good and faithful shepherd of the Gospel-flock,
him hath God chosen to guard the people of God:
to feed with divine doctrines his own folk,
for whose sake, after Christ's example, he disregardeth his life.

Quem
Him, for his merits, hath the Saviour advanced to be pontiff,
to exhort the clergy in their heavenly warfare:
to them he distributeth heavenly food with clothing,
and this is supplied in his divine and sacred discourses.

Regis
As the King's messenger bidding believers to the marriage,
he is adorned, clad in a wedding garment:
in heavenly vessels he draweth out heavenly wine;
offering drink to God's folk in the spiritual cup.

Sacrum
In the Sacred Volume sacred treasure he findeth;
and in the Saviour's flesh discerneth Deity:
this treasure he buyeth with his holy and perfect merits;
Israel is his soul's name, as 'seeing God'.

Testis

The Lord's faithful witness in the Catholic law,
his words are seasoned with the divine oracles:
lest human flesh decay, and of worms be eaten;
but with heavenly savour be salted as a sacrifice (*ad victimam*).

Verus

The true and eminent tiller of the Gospel-field,
his seeds are seen to be the Gospels of Christ:
these, with divine mouth, he soweth in the ears of the prudent,
whose hearts and minds he ploweth up with the Holy Spirit.

Xtus

Christ hath chosen him for himself to be his vicar in earth;
from twofold slavery he doth set captives free:
very many he hath redeemed from slavery to men;
countless numbers he releaseth from the Devil's thrall.

Ymnos

Hymns, with the Apocalypse and the Psalms of God, he singeth,
and doth expound the same for the edifying of God's people:
this law he holdeth in the Trinity of the Sacred Name,
and teacheth One Substance in Three Persons.

Zona

Girded with the Lord's girdle, day and night,
without intermission he prayeth unto God, the Lord:
hereafter to receive the reward of his mighty labour,
as a saint, he shall reign with the Apostles over Israel.

St Senchnall
The Writings of St Patrick, 1918
Translated by Newport J.D. White

Fiacc's 'Hymn on the Life of St. Patrick'

Patrick was born at Emptur:
This it is that history relates to us.
A child of sixteen years (was he)
When he was taken into bondage.

Succat was his name, it is said;
Who was his father is thus told:
He was son of Calpurn, son of Otidus,
Grandson of Deochain Odissus.

He was six years in slavery;
Human food he ate it not.
Cothraige he was called,
For as slave he served four families.

Victor said to Milcho's slave:
'Go thou over the sea':
He placed his foot upon the *leac* (stone):
Its trace remains, it wears not away.

He sent him across all the Alps;
Over the sea marvellous was his course,
Until he stayed with Germanus in the south,
In southern Letha.

In the islands of the Tyrrhene Sea he stayed;
Therein he meditated:
He read the canon with Germanus:
It is this that history relates.

To Ireland he was brought back
In visions by the angels of God:

Often was he in vision
Solicited to return thither again.

Salvation to Ireland
Was the coming of Patrick to Fochlaidh;
Afar was heard the sound
Of the call of the youths of Caill-Fochladh.

They prayed that the saint would come,
That he would return from Letha,
To convert the people of Erin
From error to life.

The Tuatha of Erin were prophesying
That a new kingdom of faith would come,
That it would last for evermore:
The land of Tara would be waste and silent.

The druids of Loegaire concealed not from him
The coming of Patrick;
Their prophecy was verified
As to the kingdom of which they spoke.

Patrick walked in piety till his death:
He was powerful in the extirpation of sin:
He raised his hands in blessing
Upon the tribes of men.

Hymns, and the Apocalypse, and the thrice fifty (psalms)
He was wont to sing;
He preached, baptized and prayed;
From the praise of God he ceased not.

The cold of the weather deterred him not
From passing the night in ponds:

By heaven his kingdom was protected;
He preached by day on the hills.

In Slan, in the territory of Benna-Bairche,
Hunger or thirst possessed him not.
Each night he sang a hundred psalms,
To adore the King of angels.

He slept on a bare stone,
And a wet sack-cloth around him;
A bare rock was his pillow;
He allowed not his body to be in warmth.

He preached the Gospel to all;
He wrought great miracles in Letha;
He healed the lame and the lepers;
The dead he restored to life.

Patrick preached to the Scoti:
He endured great toil in Letha:
With him will come to judgement
Everyone whom he brought to the life of Faith.

The sons of Emer, the sons of Eremon,
All went to Cisal,
To the abode of Satan –
They were swallowed up in the deep abyss,

Until the apostle came to them:
He came despite the raging tempests:
He preached, for three-score years,
The cross of Christ to the tribes of Feni.

On the land of Erin there was darkness;
The Tuatha adored the *sidhi*;

They believed not
In the true Deity of the true Trinity.

In Armagh there is sovereignty;
It is long since Emain passed away;
A great church is Dun-Lethglasse;
I wish not that Tara should be a desert.

Patrick, when he was in sickness,
Desired to go to Armagh:
An angel went to meet him on the road
In the middle of the day.

Patrick came southwards towards Victor;
He it was that went to meet him;
The bush in which Victor was, was in a blaze;
From the flame (the angel) spoke.

He said: Thy dignity (shall be) at Armagh;
Return thanks to Christ;
To heaven thou shalt come;
Thy prayer is granted thee.

The hymn which thou chosest in life
Shall be corselet of protection to all.
Around thee on the Day of Judgement
The men of Erin will come for judgement.

Tassach remaineth after him (in Sabhall),
Having given the communion to him:
He said that Patrick would return:
The word of Tassach was not false.

He (St. Patrick) put an end to night;
Light ceased not with him:

To a years' end there was radiance;
It was a long day of peace.

At the battle fought around Beth-horon
Against the Canaanites by the son of Nun,
The sun stood still at Gaboan;
This it is that the Scripture tells us.

The sun lasted with Josue unto the death of the wicked:
This indeed was befitting;
It was more befitting that there should be radiance
At the death of the saints.

The clergy of Erin went from every part
To watch around Patrick;
The sound of harmony fell upon them,
So that they slept enchanted on the way.

Patrick's body from his soul
Was severed after pains;
The angels of God on the first night
Kept choir around it unceasingly.

When Patrick departed (from life)
He went to visit the other Patrick;
Together they ascended
To Jesus, Son of Mary.

Patrick, without arrogance or pride,
Great was the good which he proposed to himself,
To be in the service of Mary's son;
Happy the hour in which Patrick was born.

Fiacc
from *The Ecclesiastical Record,* 1868

Prayer to St Patrick

We invoke holy Patrick, Ireland's chief apostle.
Glorious is his wondrous name, a flame that baptized heathen;
He warred against hard-hearted wizards.
He thrust down the proud with the help of our Lord of fair
  heaven.
He purified Ireland's meadow-lands, a mighty birth.
We pray to Patrick chief apostle; his judgement hath delivered
  us in Doom from the malevolence of dark devils.
God be with us, together with the prayer of Patrick, chief
  apostle.

Anon.
1000 Years of Irish Poetry, 1947
Translated by Whitley Stokes and John Strachan

Muirchú's *Life of Saint Patrick*

The Birth of St Patrick and his Captivity in Ireland

Patrick, also named Sochet, a Briton by race, was born in
Britain. His father was Cualfarnius, a deacon, the son (as Patrick
himself says) of a priest, Potitus, who hailed from Bannavem
Thaburniae, a place not far from our sea. This place, as I am
informed beyond hesitation or doubt, is (now) Ventre. His
mother's name was Concessa. As a boy of sixteen he was taken
captive together with others, was brought to this barbarian
island, and was held in servitude by a harsh pagan king. He
served him for six years, as is the Hebrew law, with fear of God
and trembling (in the words of the Psalmist), with many vigils
and prayers – he would pray a hundred times during the day
and a hundred times during the night giving gladly to God
what is God's and to Caesar what is Caesar's, and beginning to

fear God and love the almighty Lord; for until then he had not known the true God, but now the spirit in him was fervent. After many hardships which he endured in that country – hunger and thirst, cold and nakedness – having tended sheep, having enjoyed the frequent visits of the angelic Victoricus sent to him by God, having worked miracles, as almost all people know, having received divine messages, of which I shall quote only one or two by way of example: 'It is well that you fast; you shall soon go home to your country' and again: 'See, your ship is ready' – which, however, was not near but about two hundred miles away, where he had never been: after all these things, as we have said, which hardly anyone can enumerate, he left the pagan ruler with his deeds, entrusted himself to the holy company of eternal God in heaven, and, following the divine command, at the age of twenty-three, sailed in the ship that was awaiting him, together with strangers – aliens and pagans, who worshipped many false gods – to Britain …

And again, after many years, he was taken captive by strangers. There on the first night he was granted to hear a divine message saying to him: 'Two months you shall be with them', that is, with your enemies. And so it happened. On the sixtieth day the Lord rescued him from their hands, and provided for him and for his companions food and fire and dry weather every day until on the tenth day they met people.

And again, after a few years, he stayed, as before, happily in his own country with his relatives, who received him as their son and urged him never again to go away from them after so many trials and hardships. He, however, did not consent, and there he saw many visions.

At that time he was already approaching the age of thirty, reaching, according to the Apostle, perfect manhood, the full maturity of the age of Christ. He set out to visit and honour the apostolic see, the head, that is, of all the churches in the whole world, in order to learn and understand and practise divine wisdom and the holy mysteries to which God had called him, and in order to preach and bring divine grace to the peoples beyond the Empire, converting them to belief in Christ.

So he crossed the sea to the south of Britain and began to travel through Gaul, with the ultimate goal, as was his ardent wish, to cross the Alps (and to proceed to Rome). But on his way he found a very holy man of approved faith and doctrine, bishop of the city of Auxerre, leader of almost all Gaul, the great lord Germanus. With him he stayed for a considerable time, as Paul sat at the feet of Gamaliel, and there, in perfect subjection, patience, and obedience, he learned, loved, and practised knowledge, wisdom, chastity, and every good disposition of spirit and soul, as was his heart's desire, with great fear and love of God, in goodness and simplicity of heart, a virgin in body and in spirit.

After he had spent a long time there – some say forty years, others say thirty – his faithful friend of old, named Victoricus, who had foretold him everything as it was to happen when he was a slave in Ireland, came to him frequently in visions and told him the time had come for him to go out and fish with the net of the Gospel the wild and alien people to whom God had sent him as a teacher; and there it was said to him in a vision: 'The sons and daughters of the Wood of Fochloth are calling you', etc.

Now that the right moment had come he set out, with God's help for the work for which he had prepared himself all that time, that is, the work of the Gospel. And Germanus sent with him a senior, the priest Segitius, so as to have as companion a witness, because until then he had not yet been consecrated a bishop by the holy lord Germanus. They knew for certain that Palladius, archdeacon of Pope Celestine, the bishop of Rome, who was then occupying the apostolic see as the forty-fifth successor of St. Peter the apostle, had been consecrated and sent to this island in the cold north in order to convert it. But he was prevented from doing so (by the fact that) nobody can receive anything from the earth unless it be given him from heaven. Neither were these wild and harsh men inclined to accept his teaching nor did he himself wish to spend a long time in a foreign country, but (decided to) return to him who had sent him. On his way back from here, having crossed the first sea and begun his journey by land, he ended his life in the territory of the Britons.

On receiving the news of the death in Britain of holy Palladius – the disciples of Palladius, Augustine, Benedict, and others, on their way home had reported his decease at Ebmoria – Patrick and those who were with him made a detour and went to an admirable man and great bishop named Amathorex, who was living in a place not far away, and there holy Patrick, knowing what was to happen to him, had the episcopal grade conferred on him by the holy bishop Amathorex; also Auxilius, Iserninus and others (were ordained to) lower grades on the same day as holy Patrick was consecrated. They received blessings, performed everything according to custom, and – as if it were done specially, and aptly so, for Patrick – they sang the verse of the Psalmist: 'Thou art a priest for ever in the succession of Melchisedech.' The venerable traveller, then, in the name of the Holy Trinity, boarded a ship that was ready for him, arrived in Britain, and then, avoiding all delay that was not required by the ordinary conditions of travel – for nobody seeks the Lord with sloth – speedily and with a favourable wind sailed across our sea.

In the days when this took place there was in those parts a great king, a fierce pagan, an emperor of non-Romans, with his royal seat at Tara, which was then the capital of the realm of the Irish, by name Loíguire son of Níall, a scion of the family that held the kingship of almost the entire island. He had around him sages and druids, fortune-tellers and sorcerers, and the inventors of every evil craft, who, according to the custom of paganism and idolatry, were able to know and foresee everything before it happened. There were two of these whom he preferred above all the others, whose names are these: Lothroch, also called Lochru, and Lucet Máel, also called Ronal; and these two, by their magical art, prophesied frequently that a foreign way of life was about to come to them, a kingdom, as it were, with an unheard-of and burdensome teaching, brought from afar over the seas, enjoined by few, received by many; it would be honoured by all, would overthrow kingdoms, kill the kings who offered resistance, seduce the crowds, destroy all their gods, banish all the works of their craft, and reign for ever. They also described the man who was to bring this way of life and to win them for it, and they prophesied about him in the following words, in the form, as it were, of a poem, which these men often recited, and especially during the two or three years immediately before the coming of Patrick. These are the words of the poem – not very intelligible, owing to the peculiarity of their language:

There shall arrive Shaven-head,
with his stick bent in the head,
from his house with a hole in its head
he will chant impiety
from his table in the front of his house;
all his people will answer 'Be it thus, be it thus'.

Muirchú moccu Machtheni
from *The Vita Sanctii Patricii*
Translated by Ludwig Bieler

Jocelin's *Life and Acts of Saint Patrick*

The Proeme of Jocelin

It has been, from ancient times, the object and the design of most writers to perpetuate, with a pen worthy of their virtues, the lives of holy men, that the fervor of sanctity so deserving our veneration might not be buried in oblivion, but rather that it might shine before all as in a glass, to the end that posterity might imitate its brightness.

Wherefore, in reading the lives and acts of the saints composed in a rude manner or barbarous dialect, disgust is often excited, and not seldom tardiness of belief. And hence it is that the life of the most glorious priest Patrick, the patron and apostle of Ireland, so illustrious in signs and miracles, being frequently written by illiterate persons, through the confusion and obscurity of the style, is by most people neither liked nor understood, but is held in weariness and contempt. Charity therefore urging us, we will endeavor, by reducing them to order, to collect what are confused, when collected to compose them into a volume, and, when composed, to season them, if not with all the excellence of our language, at least with some of its elegance. To this our endeavor the instruction of the threefold instrument which is described to belong to the candlestick of the tabernacle giveth aid; for we find therein the tongs, the extinguisher, and the oil-cruse, which we must properly use, if, in describing the lives of the saints, who shone in their conversation and example like the candlestick before the Lord, we should labor to clear away the superfluous, extinguish the false, and illuminate the obscure, which, though by the devotion we have toward St. Patrick we are bound to do, yet are we thereto enjoined by the commands of the most reverend Thomas, Archbishop of Armagh and Primate of all Ireland, and of Malachy, the Bishop of Down; and to these are added the request of John de Courcy, the most illustrious Prince of Uldia, who is known to be the most especial admirer and honorer of St. Patrick.

How Saint Patrick was Carried into Ireland

As, according to the testimony of Holy Writ, the furnace tries gold and the fire of tribulation proves the just, so did the hour of his trial draw near to Patrick, that he might the more provedly receive the crown of life. For when the illustrious boy had perlustrated three lustres, already attaining his sixteenth year, he was, with many of his countrymen, seized by the pirates who were ravaging those borders, and was made captive and carried into Ireland, and was there sold as a slave to a certain pagan prince named Milcho, who reigned in the northern part of the island, even at the same age in which Joseph is recorded to have been sold into Egypt. But Joseph, being sold as a slave, and being after his humiliation exalted, received power and dominion over

A page from Jocelin's *Life and Acts of St Patrick*

all Egypt. Patrick, after his servitude and his affliction, obtained the primacy of the especial and spiritual dominion of Ireland. Joseph refreshed with corn the Egyptians oppressed by famine; Patrick, in process of time, fed with the salutary food of the Christian faith the Irish perishing under idolatry. To each was affliction sent for the profit of his soul, as is the flail to the grain, the furnace to the gold, the file to the iron, the wine-press to the grape, and the oil-press to the olive. Therefore it was that Patrick, at the command of the forementioned prince, was appointed to the care of the swine, and under his care the herd became fruitful and exceedingly multiplied. From whence it may well be learned that as the master's substance is often increased and improved by the attention of a diligent and fortunate servant or steward, so, on the other hand, is it reduced and injured under an idle or unprosperous hand. But the holy youth, heartily embracing in his soul the judgments of the Lord, made of his necessity a virtue, and, having in his office of a swineherd obtained solitude, worked out his own salvation. For he abode in the mountains, and in the woods, and in the caves of the wilderness, and having leisure for prayer, and knowing how kind was the Lord, freely and more freely did he pour forth the incense of his supplications in the presence of the Most High; and an hundred times in the day and an hundred times in the night did he on his bended knees adore his Creator, and often did he pray for a long time fasting, and, nourishing himself with the roots of herbs and with the lightest food, did he mortify his members which were stretched upon the earth. Nor him could heat, nor cold, nor snow, nor hail, nor ice, nor any other inclemency of the air compel from his spiritual exercises. Therefore went he forward daily increasing and confirming himself more strong in the faith and love of Christ Jesus; and the more weak and infirm he appeared, so much the steadier and more powerful was he in fulfilling the commands of the Lord …

How St. Patrick was Redeemed from Slavery

And Patrick went to the place which the angel had pointed out unto him, and he found therein no small weight of gold. Wherefore he addressed for his ransom his hard and cruel master, and with the offering of the yellow metal induced his mind, greedy of gold, to grant unto him his freedom. Therefore, being by the aid of Mammon solemnly released from his servitude, he went his way rejoicing, and hastened toward the sea, desiring to return to his own country. But Milcho repented that he had dismissed a servant so very necessary unto, and, falsifying his agreement, pursued Patrick that he might bring him back and reduce him to his former slavery, as Pharao pursued the Hebrews. But by the divine will, wandering both in his mind and in his course, he found not him whom he sought. Foiled, therefore, in his attempt, he returned with grief and with shame. And his sorrow was much increased, for that not only Patrick, having obtained his freedom, had escaped, but the gold which was the price of his freedom, on returning home, he found not. And with this the law accords; for to him who has served six years in slavery, the law directs that in the seventh year shall his freedom be restored ...

How he Journeyed unto Rome, and was made a Bishop; and of Palladius, the Legate of Ireland

The God of our salvation having prospered Patrick's journey, he arrive at the city which is the capital of the world; and often, with due devotion, visiting the memorials of the apostles and the martyrs, he obtained the notice and the friendship of the chief Pontiff, and found favor in his sight. In the apostolic chair then sat Pope Celestine, of that name the first, but from the blessed Apostle Peter the forty-third; but he, keeping Saint Patrick with him, and finding him perfect and approved in faith, in learning, and in holiness, at length consecrated him a bishop, and determined to send him to the conversion of the Irish nation. But Celestine had sent before him, for the sake of preaching in Ireland, another doctor named Palladius, his archdeacon, to whom, with his coadjutors, he gave many books, the two Testaments, with the relics of the Apostles Peter and Paul and of numberless martyrs; and the Irish not listening to, but rather obstinately opposing, Palladius in his mission, he quitted their country, and, going towards Rome, died in Britain, near the borders of the Picts; yet, while in Scotland, converting some to the faith of Christ, he baptized them and founded three churches built of oak, in which he left as prelates his disciples Augustine, Benedict, Sylvester, and Sulomus, with the parchments and the relics of the saints which he had collected. To him with more profitable labor did Saint Patrick succeed, as is said in the Irish proverb, 'Not to Palladius, but to Patrick, the Lord vouchsafed the conversion of Ireland.' And the Pope, being certified of Palladius's death, immediately gave to Patrick the command, which hitherto, keeping more secret counsel, he had delayed, to proceed on his journey and on the salutary work of his legation.

Jocelin
Life and Acts of Saint Patrick
Translated by Edmund L. Swift
The Most Ancient Lives of Saint Patrick, 1874

Events in Connexion with the Religious History of Ireland

AD 50	The Apostle John preaches to the Asiatic Celts.
AD 120	Polycarp, the disciple of John, is supposed to have preached Christ effectively to the Gauls.
AD 160	(or thereabouts) The Christian religion had made way in Ireland, chiefly by missionaries from Gaul.
AD 250	Cormac, an Irish King, embraced Christianity, and a number of his subjects.

AD 300	Several of the clergymen of Britain fled to Ireland, to avoid persecution, and greatly helped the cause of the Gospel.
AD 372	Patrick born at Taberna, near Dumbarton.
AD 387	Nial, the Irish King, makes a raid upon North Britain, and brings Patrick, among others, to Ireland.
AD 387–392	Patrick herds cattle and sheep for Milcho, in the Braid, Parish of Rathcavin and Skerry.
AD 412	(or thereabouts) Patrick, having studied for the ministry in Gaul, returns to Ireland, and enters upon his evangelical labours in the Counties of Down and Antrim.
AD 465	On 17th March, Patrick dies near Dundrum, and is supposed to be interred at Downpatrick.
AD 560	Columkill, a native of County Donegal, and a most learned and eminent minister, founded a College at Iona, from whence missionaries were sent to different parts of the British Isles. About the same time, Comgall, a native of Larne, founded a College at Bangor, which was for many centuries a famous seat of learning.
AD 670	The Irish clergy refused to be reordained by the English Bishops.
AD 800–1010	The Danes oppressed and plundered the Irish people, and assisted the English Prelates, in introducing Roman Catholic usages into the country.
AD 1139	Pope's Legate received in Ireland for the first time.
AD 1140	Monks first introduced into Ireland.
AD 1151	The Synod of Kells enforces the celibacy of the Irish clergy, which had not hitherto been a rule.
AD 1160	The Pope hands over Ireland to be conquered by Henry II, on consideration of his advancing the

interest of the Roman Catholic Church in the country.

AD 1172   Ireland conquered. The Council of Cashel meets, and decrees strict uniformity between the Irish Church and the system at Rome.

AD 1360   Wickliffe preaches in England, and translates the Scriptures into the English tongue. About the same time, Fitzraph of Dundalk, translates part of the Scriptures into the *Irish* language.

AD 1535   The Reformation in England and Ireland, encouraged by Henry VIII.

AD 1541   Doctor Browne, a learned and devoted clergyman, was appointed Protestant Archbishop of Dublin.

AD 1547   Edward VI ascended the throne, and greatly encouraged the Reformation in England and Ireland. Cranmer and his brethren assisted zealously in the good work.

AD 1556   Romanism being restored under Queen Mary, Dean Cole is sent to Dublin, with the Queen's letter, empowering the authorities to persecute the Protestants. Whilst enjoying himself in an Inn in Chester, he lets out the fact of the persecuting document being in a small box. Eliza Edmonds, the landlady of the Inn, who had a brother in Dublin that was a Protestant, took out the offensive paper and put a pack of cards in its place. Before another Royal Letter could be procured, Queen Mary had gone to her account. Queen Elizabeth is said to have settled £40 a year upon Eliza Edmonds for life.

AD 1558   Elizabeth ascended the throne, and took measures to secure the profession of the Reformed faith.

AD 1580   English and Scottish families began to settle in Ulster.

AD 1613	Scottish ministers came over, and took charge of congregations made up of colonists.
AD 1642	The first Irish Presbytery was formed at Carrickfergus.
AD 1620–56	Archbishop Ussher and Bishop Bedell labored with exemplary zeal for the enlightenment of the Irish Roman Catholics.

John Armstrong
*Saint Patrick, A Protestant, and an Early Promoter of True
  Religion in Ireland, Especially Ulster, 1859*

Patrick

The little Princesses, Ethna and Fedelma, were the daughters of the King of Connaught. They were quite young, indeed little more than children, and full of fun and life. In the summer months, when the weather was hot, they used to begin the day with a bathe. The place they bathed in was near the palace, yet it was quite private, and no one ever came near it early in the morning.

One day Ethna and Fedelma and their two maids-in-waiting got a surprise: there were a whole lot of tents set out on the grassy slope near their bathing pool. They stared, then they listened; there was a droning of voices, and the language was a strange one. Every now and again a voice broke into song – and very sweet it was, mingled with the bird song from the nearby woods and the water sound from the river.

Saint Patrick and his companions had come and were saying the Divine Office in Latin. They had arrived during the night and they had a message for the King of Connaught. They, of course, knew nothing of princesses taking daily bathes, and the princesses knew nothing at all about Patrick and his companions, because they were poor pagans.

The voices stopped and a man came out into the open. He was a small man but very strongly made; he looked like a man who spent all his days and nights in the open. It was Saint Patrick.

Girls and man stared at one another. Then one of the girls said, rather severely: 'Who are you, and where do you come from?'

Patrick did not answer for some seconds. Then he said: 'We have more important things to tell you than just our names and where we come from. We know who the one true God is whom you should adore …'

Some might say that the man did not answer the princesses very politely. He brushed aside their questions and went on to something quite different. But far from being annoyed, the young girls were delighted. In a flash something seemed to light up inside them, to make a blinding white blaze in their hearts and minds. They knew at once that this was real, real news and that it was as true as night and day, true as being alive. It all happened in a few seconds. Then they asked questions – a whole torrent of questions:

'Who is God? Where does He live? Will He live for ever? Will we see Him and be with Him when we die? Who is His Son? Is Christ beautiful? What are we to do?'

Patrick answered all their questions, quickly and simply. He, too, was delighted: the light that lit up in the girls was in the man also and the three lights together made one tremendous light. The maids and Saint Patrick's companions stood around listening to the quick questions and the lovely answers; they knew that they were very lucky to be near the saintly man and the sweet girls, and they felt that the Holy Ghost was there, too, in their midst.

'Oh, tell us how to find the good God. Teach us more about the kind Christ who died on the Cross. Tell us more, more, more,' the two princesses kept saying. But there was not any great need to tell them more: they had already received the Spirit of Truth. Patrick led them to the pool where each morning they went to bathe, and there he baptized them. For a little while after, Ethna and Fedelma were very quiet; they asked no questions; they were praying. Patrick prepared to say Mass; his companions got an altar ready. Then the girls came to him again.

'I want to *see* Jesus Christ,' said Ethna.

'And so do I,' said Fedelma. 'I want to be with Him in His home for ever and ever.'

Eileen Coghlan

Patrick was very moved by this loving longing. Very gently he told them that that was impossible, that they would not be able to see God until after death. They were young, he told them, and had their lives to live, and if they lived Christian lives they would then go to God for always and always, and great joys would take the place of the sorrows of this world. The girls said no more, and Patrick began the Mass.

The Mass went on. The water seemed to sing as it flowed by, an odd bird chirruped, a wind rustled the leaves in the trees. Everyone was still. Then the youngest man in the company rang a little bell and all bowed their heads. Jesus Christ was with them in the grassy place beside the water in the King of Connaught's park. Soon the bell rang again: it was the Communion of the Mass. Patrick turned around with the vessel of Sacred Hosts and, beckoning to the King's daughters, he gave them Holy Communion.

For a little while the girls looked so happy and so beautiful that they were like angels. And then (the story tells us) they died. They longed so much to be with Christ that they died of longing. We don't know – and we will never know until we die ourselves – why God took those young girls, but He must have loved them very much to have done so. We do know, however, how happy Saint Patrick was to have met with such quick and whole-hearted, whole-souled belief. When he had to take the road again – the hard unkind road that went up and down Ireland – his step was light and there was a smile on his lips.

Alice Curtayne
Irish Saints for Boys and Girls, 1955

To Which Church Did Saint Patrick Belong?

There is hardly any Church to-day that has not claimed to have a special property in the Irish Apostle. The Church of Rome asserts an exclusive claim to him, and turns a deaf ear to the numerous voices and evidences that go to invalidate that claim. The Protestant-Episcopalian also affirms an exclusive ownership, so that both the Armagh Primates are alike strenuous and confident in tracing their ecclesiastical lineage to St Patrick. It has been maintained by some that he was a Presbyterian, while a voluminous work has appeared assigning reasons which convince the author that our Irish national apostle was a Baptist. All such pretensions seem to us vain and futile. The fact is that the Church planted in Ireland by St Patrick was absolutely unique, differing in many and important features from any church now existing, and in no church now extant do we find its exact image, or anything approaching it, reflected.

Anon.
Reprinted with alterations from *The Christian Irishman*, 1906

The Church in Irish Society

When Christianity reached Ireland in the fifth century it came from different sources, from Britain and from the Continent … Patrick came from Roman Britain, though his own education was interrupted and his command of Latin exiguous … The Pelagian controversy shows us a body of educated Christians in Britain in the first half of the fifth century … Patrick's own education was very different from Pelagius'. His Latin was not that of the educated reader, but a colloquial and ecclesiastical Latin. He spoke quite justifiably of his own *rusticitas*. He knew the Bible, and when its vocabulary was suited to what he has to say he is able to convey his meaning; but where he is relating everyday facts his style is so clumsy that meaning is often very difficult to grasp. Latin must have been his second language as a boy, but his captivity between the ages of 15 and 22 seriously weakened his command of Latin. He was a man of one book, and there are no traces in the 'Confession' or 'Epistle' of quotations or borrowings from any book other than the Bible.

Our records say that Palladius had come to the Irish believing in Christ before Patrick's arrival, but if so it must have been to a different part of Ireland and his mission must have had limited influence, for Patrick found no Christian Latin tradition. 'Everything in Patrick's Latin', says Mohrmann, 'points to beginning and to isolation.' The church he reflects is more or less apostolic. He uses no word for church-building. Christians are called *plebs, fideles, credentes, timentes Deum, famuli Dei, sancti.* He speaks of the sacraments of baptism, confirmation, and ordination, and of the word of preaching. His language is that of an infant church with bishops and priests and deacons, and an organisation like that of early Christian days. There are practically no monastic terms. This proves conclusively that the Irish church had not yet developed its monastic character, and that in Patrick's day it had no close relationship with southern Gaul, where monasticism was firmly established …

Patrick's own writings name no centre for his mission, but tradition locates it in the north at Armagh. This is almost certainly right. Armagh is two miles from Emain Macha, the capital of Ulster, and its foundation must pre-date the contraction of Ulster. The unsettled political history of this area in the later fifth and sixth centuries may well explain why Patrick drops out of Irish records until the seventh century.

The annals give a variety of different dates for Patrick's floruit. The Annals of Ulster at 457 give *Quies senis Patricii ut alii libri dicunt,* and again in 461 *hic alii quietem Patricii dicunt.* The Annals of Inisfallen put his death at 496, but say *anno 432 a passione Domini,* and the Annals of Ulster give it again at 491 and 492: at 491 *dicunt Scoiti hic Patricium archiepiscopum defunctum,* and at 492 that he died in the 120th year of his age, on 17 March, sixty years after coming to Ireland …

The genealogical tracts say that Emain Macha fell to the three Collas, cousins of Niall's father, but it was Niall and his sons who finally broke up the 'fifth' of Ulster. It is almost certain that the foundation of the Christian centre of Armagh must belong to the period before the final collapse of Ulster. If we date the death of Niall and the *floruit* of his sons to the second half of the fifth century we can accept the period of approximately 461–92 as a likely one for Patrick …

The 'Epistle' and 'Confession' show a first-generation missionary church. The love of Christ had given Patrick to the

Irish people, so that he was committed to serve them for the duration of his life. His position was insecure; he gave his free birth for the benefit of the Irish, suffering bonds. He speaks specifically of two periods of captivity, once for two months, when he was delivered on the sixtieth night, once in irons when he was delivered on the fourteenth day. He has preached constantly in the extremities of the world: 'We are witnesses that the gospel has been preached unto those parts beyond which there lives nobody.' He has baptized thousands and confirmed many, and clerics have been ordained for them everywhere. He repeats these claims more than once: of many baptisms, confirmations, and the installation of priests to minister to the converts.

It was not a monastic church, yet there were converts living an ascetic and celibate life … This is the picture of an active missionary church, successfully making converts, spreading its clergy; a church following a socially aristocratic routine, with a bishop accompanied by princes and distributing largesse. Patrick's own teaching must have been grounded on the scriptures, but probably on little else. He said himself: 'I have not studied like the others', and it is difficult to believe that he could have had any substantial period of training at Auxerre or any comparable centre. The 'Epistle' and 'Confession' give only a vague idea of ecclesiastical administration …

The church is a community within a still-pagan society and is to hold itself separate from the world. The alms of pagans are not to be accepted … There are other rulings that also suggest a church still in a fairly primitive state. The clerics of the diocese form a kind of college, who have to turn up at matins and vespers; yet they may be married. The church is served by bishops, priests, deacons, lectors, psalmists, ostiaries, but monks and virgins exist … It seems to me that these canons must belong to the pre-monastic church …

The first stage of Irish Christianity lasts, then, from about 400 to 500. Christianity first arrived probably in the south of Ireland.

Palladius, probably a cleric of Auxerre, arrived in 431 as the first bishop to the Irish Christians who had already established themselves … Probably in the second half of the century Patrick the Briton came to Ulster and a church was set up at Armagh near the old capital of Ulster. Emain Macha subsequently fell to the Uí Néill, the borders of Ulster were pushed eastwards, and Patrick disappeared from Irish tradition for 150 years.

Kathleen Hughes
The Church in Early Irish Society, 2005

A Possible Chronology for Saint Patrick

384   Patrick's family move from Scotland to Brittany.

385   Patrick is born in Brittany (possibly at Tours –
           Nemthor/Naem-Tour – or on the family estate at
           Bannavem Tiburniae).

401   Patrick is taken captive from Brittany.

407   Patrick escapes from slavery in Ireland.

407–411   Patrick is trained at the monastery of St Martin of Tours.

411–420   Patrick undertakes religious and spiritual formation
           with 'barefoot hermits' in the isles of the Tyrrhene Sea
           near Mont St Michel.

420–427   Patrick continues religious formation on these islands.

428   Patrick is ordained as a bishop by St Senior on Mont St
           Michel and commissioned for the Mission to Ireland.

428   Patrick returns to Ireland as an apostle.

429   St Germanus sent to Britain by Pope Celestine.

431   Palladius sent to Ireland by Pope Celestine as part
           of the first official mission from Rome (Prosper's
           Chronicle).

432   Traditional date given in the Irish annals for the
           beginning of Patrick's mission in Ireland.

Marcus Losack
Rediscovering Patrick: A New Theory of Origins, 2013

Patrick

Patrick (Patricius, Pátraic, Pádraig) (c.420–490?), patron saint of Ireland, was born into a Christian family of fifth-century Roman Britain, son of Calpornius, *decurio* and deacon, and grandson of Potitus, a priest. Nothing is known of his mother ...

Patrick is the most important figure in Irish Christian history. All that can be said about his life must be weighed against the testimony of the two brief surviving texts which he personally wrote. These are the 'Confessio' and the 'Epistola' (or 'Letter to the soldiers of Coroticus'), both as noteworthy for what they do not tell us as for what they do. Writing the 'Confessio' in his old age, Patrick defends the work of a lifetime against the allegations of detractors. The 'Epistola', probably the earlier text, is an open letter of excommunication to the soldiers of one Coroticus who have killed some of Patrick's Irish converts and enslaved others. Neither document contains any reference to absolute chronology, and Patrick's dates are a matter of inference, although no one seriously doubts the correctness of inferring a fifth-century floruit. This much is suggested by Patrick's several references to a background in Britain which can be characterised as late Roman, and by his reference to the ransoming of captives from pagan Franks – a people progressively Christianised following the conversion of Clovis *c.*496 ...

But Patrick gives no indication that his work was easy and refers often in the 'Confessio' to the burden of his commission.

He says nothing of Palladius, the continental deacon, perhaps from Poitiers, who in 431 was appointed 'to the Irish believing in Christ' by Pope Celestine, 'as their first bishop', as the chronicle of Prosper of Aquitaine records. This carries the crucial implication that there were Christians in Ireland before Palladius (or Patrick) arrived, as indeed the evidence of ogham suggests. What happened to Palladius is not recorded, but Muirchú, writing a life of Patrick in the seventh century, maintains that he failed in his endeavours and soon left the country to return to Rome, dying in Britain en route. Accordingly, the Irish annals retrospectively place Patrick's arrival at 432. But there is evidence in a further observation by Prosper and in a sermon delivered by Pope Leo the Great in 441 that Palladius's mission had been a success and had included some element of evangelism. If so, his sphere of operations was presumably Leinster, where later tradition places his few foundations. There is much to recommend the thesis, first advanced by J.H. Todd (1864) and elaborated by T.F. O'Rahilly (1942), that the *acta* of Palladius were absorbed by the cult of Patrick. The same process may have given rise to the inordinately long or Mosaic life-span with which Patrick was sometimes credited, and to the tradition of his training at Auxerre (a place with which Palladius was associated). The debt of Irish Christianity to Rome was acknowledged in the 590s by Columbanus in a letter to the pope in which he probably had Palladius in mind.

Patrick's appointment cannot have been papal, or he would surely have said so, and by his own testimony his mission was to the unconverted. This motivation would have met with little official sympathy, given that organised missions to evangelise non-Christians formed no part of the fifth-century papal agenda, although conversions were welcomed when otherwise achieved. Patrick emerges as an innovator, even a radical, driven by a desire to take the gospel 'as far as where there is no one beyond' ('Confessio', 34) and to bring to fulfilment in his own person biblical prophecies of the Last Days. Patrick embodies, or exemplifies by implication, the prophecy of Joel that in the Last Days 'your young men shall see visions, and your old men shall dream dreams' (Acts 2:17), for he himself in both youth and maturity was guided by visions and dreams. His purpose in invoking their authority in the 'Confessio' is to defend his life's work against a series of accusations emanating, it seems, from the seniors of the church in Roman Britain.

Cormac Bourke
Dictionary of Irish Biography, 2009

The Living Memory of St. Patrick

If we ask ourselves what place St. Patrick holds in the spiritual and cultural life of Ireland today, the answer will not come without hesitation. St. Patrick is the patron of the metropolitan See of Armagh, of Dublin's second (now Protestant) cathedral, and of Ireland's most illustrious Catholic college; numerous churches are dedicated to him not only in the land of his mission but in all those parts of the world which attracted Irish missionaries in the Middle Ages or Irish emigrants in modern times. His name is one of the commonest Christian names among the Irish both at home and abroad; it still clings to many places in Celtic lands and even to some in other districts of Europe. Speakers of Gaelic commemorate their apostle many times a day in a traditional greeting. His statue is found in every church where Irish Catholics go for prayer, and his feast is celebrated as a national holiday. St. Patrick is indeed the national hero of Christian Ireland.

Ludwig Bieler
The Life and Legend of St. Patrick: Problems of Modern Scholarship, 1948

The Teaching of St. Patrick

The nature and content of St. Patrick's religious belief and practice may be gathered partly from his own writings, and partly from what we know of the doctrine accepted by the Church of the West in the early part of the fifth century A.D.

St. Patrick's extant writings are his *Confession* and his *Letter*. These are both in Latin, and seem to have been written near the close of his life – not earlier than A.D. 450; he died in A.D. 461. To these undoubtedly genuine works we may add the ancient Irish hymn known as *St. Patrick's Breastplate*, and four Latin *Sayings*, preserved in the *Book of Armagh* …

There is one passage in the *Confession*, which at first sight looks like a formal creed; it runs thus:

> There is no other God, nor was there ever any in times past, nor shall there be hereafter, except God the Father unbegotten, without beginning, from whom all things take their beginning, holding all things [i.e. Almighty], as we say and his Son Jesus Christ, whom we affirm verily to have always existed with the Father before the creation of the world, with the Father after the manner of a spiritual existence, begotten ineffably before the beginning of anything. And by him were made things visible and invisible. He was made mad; and, having overcome death, he was received up into heaven to the Father. And he gave to him all power above every name of things in heaven and things in earth and things under the earth; and let every tongue confess to him that Jesus Christ is Lord and God, in whom we believe. And we look for this coming soon to be; he the Judge of the quick and the dead, who will render to every man according to his deeds. And he shed on us abundantly the Holy Ghost, the gift and

earnest of immortality who makes them to believe and obey to become children of God the Father, and joint heirs with Christ, whom we confess and adore as one God in the Trinity of the Holy Name.

In view of the fact that the Celtic Churches were sound in the faith as to the Godhead and the Incarnation, we must hold that the omission in this passage of several clauses in the Creeds of Nicaea (A.D. 325) and of Constantinople (A.D. 381) is not due to heresy on St. Patrick's part. We know now that the basis of this section of the *Confession* is a passage from a Commentary on the Revelation by Victorinus, Bishop of Pettau [a town in Jugo-Slavia] (martyred under the emperor Diocletian, A.D. 303–313). We learn from St. Sechnall's *Hymn in Patrick's Praise* that Patrick was a diligent student and expounder of the book of Revelation.

We have here then, not a formal creed, but St. Patrick's declaration of his doctrine of God. The doctrine of the Holy Trinity was, he tells, (*Conf.*), his *Rule of Faith* ...

One of the most noticeable elements in the personal life of St. Patrick, as reflected in his writings, was the intensity of his devotion to our Lord Jesus Christ. He speaks of him as 'Christ my Lord', 'Christ my God', 'Christ the Lord'. A specially striking passage is in *Confessions*, an account of a vision:– 'Whether within me, or beside me, I cannot tell, God knoweth ... at the end of the prayer he thus affirmed, "He who laid down his life for thee, he it is who speaketh in these."' This sense of the mutual indwelling of Christ and the human soul finds its supreme expression in the *Breastplate*:

Christ with me, Christ beside me,
Christ behind me, Christ in me,
Christ under me, Christ over me,
Christ to right of me, Christ to left of me,
Christ in lying down, Christ in sitting, Christ in rising up,

Christ in the heart of every person, who may think of me!
Christ in the mouth of every one, who may speak to me!
Christ in every eye, which may look on me!
Christ in every ear, which may hear me!

St. Patrick knew of only 'one mediator between God and man, Christ Jesus': for him the only intercessors with God for man are Jesus Christ and the Holy Spirit.

As regard the state of the soul between death and the Judgment Day, St. Patrick speaks only of Hell and Paradise. Individual thinkers had suggested that there might possibly be an intermediate state in which such Christians as do not seem good enough to go straight to Hell, might gradually be cleansed from the stain of sin. But no authoritative declaration that there is a Purgatory was made until Pope Gregory the Great (died A.D. 604) affirmed it.

Indulgences, in the sense of remission, after death, of the punishment for sin, depend upon the doctrine of Purgatory; and were, of course, unknown in St. Patrick's time.

St. Patrick is a witness to the Apostolic three 'Orders of Ministers in Christ's Church: Bishops, Priests, and Deacons'. He speaks of himself as 'a bishop, appointed by God, in Ireland' (*Letter*) and refers more than once to the episcopal functions of Ordination and Confirmation; the duties of the clergy (*clerics*) generally being to baptize and exhort the people.

The second order of Ministers he terms either *presbyteri* or *sacerdotes*. In the two places in which the latter word occurs, the 'sacerdotal' functions specified are (a) public admonition of the people, and (b) the power of 'declaring to God's people, being penitent, the absolution and remission of their sins' …

The 'secular', or parish, clergy in Britain and Ireland were not compelled to be unmarried until some centuries later than St. Patrick's time. He himself states, without any comment, that his own father was a deacon and his grandfather a presbyter. On the other hand, the ideal for a Christian life which he set before his converts was that they should become 'monks and virgins of Christ'. The unreasonable notion that a pure unmarried life is, essentially, more pleasing to God than is a pure married life was strongly advocated by the Church leaders of the fourth century: and we cannot be surprised if St. Patrick shared in the opinions of those whom he venerated ...

Prominence is given to St. Patrick's writings to the sacrament of Holy Baptism and to Confirmation. It is not clear whether the unction alluded to in the *Letter* was administered in connection with Baptism or whether the unction is that of Confirmation, which in this instance followed the baptism almost immediately.

But the only reference in these writings to the sacrament of Holy Communion is in *Confession*, where, describing the enthusiasm of the 'devout women' among his converts, he says, 'They used to cast off their ornaments upon the altar'. We know that in the early Celtic Church, as in the Gallican Church, the presentation of money and other precious things at the time of the Offertory was a prominent feature in the service of Holy Communion ...

In the absence of any statement by St. Patrick himself, it is reasonable to hold that his belief and practice as to the Holy Communion were those of the Church in which he had been educated, that is the Church of Gaul, or France ...

The Eucharistic doctrine of the great divines of the fourth century – St. Patrick's elder contemporaries – St. Ambrose (died A.D. 397) and St. Augustine (died A.D. 430) was the same as those of our *Book of Common Prayer*. They taught that by his 'death upon the Cross' our Lord made 'a full, perfect and sufficient sacrifice ... for the sins of the whole world', and that the service of Holy Communion is 'a perpetual memory' or memorial, of that one sacrifice, which itself can never be repeated. This is St. Paul's teaching, in I Cor. xi. 26, 'Ye proclaim the Lord's death fill he come.' By partaking of the bread and wine, after they have been consecrated by Christ, acting through the minister of his Church, his body (I Cor. x. 16), the faithful communicant – beside other benefits – shares in the merits of the sacrifice of Christ. Consequently, a consecration by the priest and a communion of the people must always go together. This was what was taught by the most venerated teachers of the Church in St. Patrick's time.

Rev. Canon N.J.D. White
The Teaching of Saint Patrick, 1932

The Pre-Patrician Spread of Christianity in Ireland

Evidence for the early and pre-Patrician spread of Christianity in Ireland comes from various sources … There are five saints, St. Declan, St. Ailbe, St. Ciaran of Saigher, St. Abban and St. Ibar, who are fairly certainly established as pre-Patricians. St. Abban mocu Corbmaic is associated with the churches of Moyarney (Mag-Arnaide) and Killabban (Cell-Abbain) in Leinster. St. Ibar was a bishop and had his chief church on Beggery Island (Becc-Eriu) in Wexford Harbour – a very likely spot for an Early Christian settlement since it is one of the south Irish ports in touch with continental Europe. No Life survives of Ibar, but he is supposed to have been the most obstinate of the clerics who opposed Patrick's work in Ireland. Patrick did not only have to convince pagans; he had to get the goodwill of the existing Christian population, who might well be expected to be suspicious of a British stranger who sought to organise their Church.

D.D.C. Pochin Mould
Ireland of the Saints, 1953

THE WRITINGS OF
ST PATRICK

The extant writings of Saint Patrick are generally acknowledged to be the *Confession of Saint Patrick*, the *Letter to Coroticus*, the *Sayings of Saint Patrick* – all written in Latin – and the *Breastplate of Saint Patrick* – written in Old Irish. These texts have been translated and interpreted by churchmen and scholars since their first appearance, because they represent the earliest sources for an understanding of the life, mission and teaching of the patron saint of Ireland.

While the *Confession* is not autobiographical, it contains important references to the life of the author. It was written by Patrick in his maturity – more likely his old age – and was, in reality, a justification of his life's work: his mission to convert the Irish to Christianity. The necessity for such a justification arose from attacks upon his mission from fellow clerics, either Irish or English; and the intended audience was primarily the Christian communities in Britain from whence Patrick had come, or to whom he owed some form of allegiance. It was also aimed at his fellow religious in Ireland.

The *Letter to Coroticus* is most likely of earlier date than the *Confession*, though by its content and style, not much earlier. It was an immediate and angry response to what was the scourge of the British Isles and Ireland in the fifth century – piracy and slave trading. Coroticus, king of that region of north Britain around Strathclyde, fitted out and sanctioned a slave raid on the coast of Ireland. Newly-baptised Christians were killed in the raid, and a number carried off into slavery by the soldiers of Coroticus. On learning of this, Patrick sent one of his trusted priests to confront Coroticus and read aloud a letter of excommunication.

The *Sayings of Saint Patrick* are first recorded in the ninth century *Book of Armagh*. They seem to be some disjointed jottings on a personal faith. As such they add something to an understanding of the faith of Saint Patrick, and in turn, suggest the nature of his ministry and preaching to the Irish.

The *Breastplate of Saint Patrick* is the only writing of the saint in the Irish language. The hymn is also known as the *Lorica of Saint Patrick* (lorica is Latin for breastplate) and the *Faeth Fiadha* (Irish for The Deer's Cry). The story is told by Muirchú in his *Life of Saint Patrick*. He relates how Patrick avoided capture and death at the hands of King Laoighre by turning himself and his followers into deer and passing from the danger. As they escaped Patrick recited the hymn of protection that he had composed.

Scholars and laymen continue to peruse these texts in their endeavour to understand the life and teachings of Saint Patrick. To these they add context by studying the contemporary political, social and ecclesiastical history of fifth-century Ireland, Britain and Europe. This style of research stems from earlier research in the nineteenth and twentieth centuries which examined Patrick's writings for his devotion to Jesus Christ and the cult of Christ, his belief in the doctrine of the Trinity and his understanding of the Bible.

The Confession of Saint Patrick

I, Patrick, a sinner, the rudest and the least of all the faithful, and most contemptible to very many, had for my father Calpornius, a deacon, a son of Potitus a presbyter, who dwelt in the village of Bannavem Taberniæ; for he had a small farm hard by the place where I was taken captive. I was then nearly sixteen years of age. I did not know the true God: and I was taken to Ireland in captivity with so many thousand men in accordance with our deserts, because we departed from God, and kept not his precepts, and were not obedient to our priests, who admonished us for our salvation.

And the Lord brought down upon us 'the wrath of His indignation', and dispersed us among many nations, even to the end of the earth, where now my littleness is seen among foreigners. And there the Lord opened (to me) the sense of my unbelief, that, though late, I might remember my sins, and that I might strengthen my whole heart to the Lord my God, who had respect to my humiliation, and pitied my youth and ignorance, and took care of me before I knew Him, and before I had wisdom, or could discern between good and evil; and protected me and comforted me as a father does a son.

Wherefore I cannot keep silent – nor is it indeed expedient (to do so) – concerning so great benefits, and so much favour as the Lord has vouchsafed to me in the land of my captivity; because this is our recompense (to Him) that after our chastening, or knowledge of God, we should exalt and confess his wonderful works before every nation which is under the whole heaven.

Because there is no other God, neither ever was, neither before, nor shall be hereafter, except the Lord the Father, unbegotten, without beginning. From whom is all beginning; Upholding all things, as we have said; And His Son Jesus Christ, whom indeed with the Father, we testify to have always been, Before the origin of the world, spiritually with the Father; In an inexplicable manner begotten before all beginning; And by himself were made the things visible and invisible; And was made man; And, death having been vanquished, was received into the heavens to the Father. And He has given to Him all power 'above every name of those that are in heaven, on earth, and under the earth, that every tongue should confess' to Him that Jesus Christ is Lord and God, In whom we believe, and expect His coming, to be ere long 'the judge of the living and of the dead', 'Who will render to everyone according to his deeds'. And He hath 'poured upon us abundantly' the Holy Spirit, a gift and pledge of immortality; Who makes the faithful and obedient to become 'sons of God, and joint-heirs with Christ'; Whom we confess and adore— one God in the Trinity of the sacred name.

For He Himself has said by the prophet, 'Call upon me in the day of thy tribulation, and I will deliver three, and thou shalt magnify me.' And again He saith, 'It is honourable to reveal and confess the words of God.'

Although I am in many respects imperfect, I wish my brethren and acquaintances to know my disposition, and that they may be able to comprehend the wish of my soul. I am not ignorant of the testimony of my Lord, who witnesses in the Psalm, 'Thou shalt destroy those that speak a lie.' And again, 'The mouth that belieth killeth the soul.' And the same Lord says in the Gospel, 'The idle word that men shall speak, they shall render an account of it in the day of judgement.' Therefore, I ought earnestly with fear and trembling to dread this sentence in that day when no one shall be able to withdraw herself, or to hide, but when we all together shall render account of even the smallest of our sins before the tribunal of the Lord Christ.

Wherefore, I thought of writing long ago, but hesitated even till now; because I feared falling into the tongue of men; because I have not learned like others who have drunk in, in the best manner, both law and sacred literature in both ways equally; and have never changed their language from infancy, but have always added more to its perfection; for our language and speech is translated into a foreign tongue.

As can be easily proved from the drivel of my writing – how I have been instructed and learned in diction; because the wise man says: 'For by the tongue is discerned understanding and knowledge, and the teaching of truth.' But what avails an excuse, although according to truth, especially when accompanied with presumption? Since indeed I myself, now in my old age, strive after what I did not learn in my youth, because they prevented me from learning thoroughly that which I had read through before. But who believes me? And if I should say, as I have already said, that when a youth, nay almost a boy in words, I was taken captive, before I knew what I ought to seek, or what I ought to aim at, or what I ought to avoid. Hence I blush to-day, and greatly fear to expose my unskillfulness, because I cannot express myself with clearness and brevity, nor even as the spirit moves and the mind and endowed understanding point out.

But if it had been granted to me even as to others, I would not however be silent because of the recompense. And if, perhaps, it appears to some, that I put myself forward in this matter with my ignorance and slower tongue, it is, however, written: 'Stammering tongues shall learn quickly to speak peace.' How much more ought we to aim at this – we who are the 'epistle of Christ' – for salvation even to the end of the earth – and if not eloquent, yet powerful and very strong – written in your hearts 'not with ink,' it is testified ... 'but by the Spirit of the living God.'

And again the Spirit testifies; 'Husbandry was ordained by the Most High.' Therefore, I, first a rustic, a fugitive, unlearned, indeed not knowing how to provide for the future – but I know this most certainly, that before I was humbled, I was like a stone lying in deep mud; and He who is mighty came, and in His mercy raised me and lifted me up, and placed me on the top of the wall. And hence I ought loudly to cry out to return also something to the Lord for his so great benefits here, and in eternity, which benefits the human mind cannot estimate. But, therefore, be ye astonished, both great and small, ye who fear God.

And ye rhetoricians, and you lords of the land, hear and examine: Who aroused me, a fool, from the midst of those who appear to be wise, and skilled in the laws, and powerful in speech and in every matter? And me – who am detested by this world – He has inspired me beyond others, (if indeed I be such) on condition, that with fear and reverence, and without complaining, faithfully to the nation – to which the love of Christ has transferred me, and given me for my life – that in fine, as long as I shall be alive, I should serve them with humility and in truth.

In the measure, therefore, of the faith of the Trinity it behoves me to distinguish without shrinking from danger, to make known the gift of God, and his 'everlasting consolation,' and fearlessly to spread faithfully everywhere the name of God, in order that even after my death to leave it to my Gallican brethren, and to my sons, whom I have baptized in the Lord – so many thousand men. And I was not worthy, nor deserving that the Lord should grant this to his servant; that after going through afflictions and so many difficulties, after captivity, after many years, He should grant me so great favour among that nation, which when I was yet in my youth I have never hoped for, nor thought of.

But after I had come to Ireland I daily used to feed cattle, and I prayed frequently during the day; the love of God and the fear of Him increased more and more, and faith became stronger, and the spirit was stirred; so that in one day I said about a hundred prayers, and in the night nearly the same; so that I used even to remain in the woods and in the mountain; before daylight I used to rise to prayer, through snow, through frost, through rain, and felt no harm; nor was there any slothfulness in me, as I now perceive, because the spirit was then fervent within me.

And there indeed one night, in my sleep, I heard a voice saying to me, 'Thou fastest well, fasting (so), thou shalt soon go to thy country.' And again, after a very short time, I heard a response saying to me, 'Behold, thy ship is ready.' And it was not near, but perhaps 200 miles away, and I never had been there, nor was I acquainted with any of the men there.

After this I took flight, and left the man with whom I had been six years; and I came in the strength of the Lord, who directed my way for good; and I feared nothing till I arrived at that ship. And on that same day on which I arrived the ship moved out of its place, and I asked them (the sailors) that I might go and sail with them. And it displeased the captain, and he answered sharply with indignation, 'Do not by any means seek to go with us.' And when I heard this, I separated myself from them to go to the hut where I lodged. And on the way I began to pray; and before I had ended my prayer, I heard one of them, and he was calling loudly after me, 'Come quickly, for these men are calling you.' And immediately I returned to them and they began to say to me, 'Come, for we receive you in good faith, make friendship with us in whatever way you wish.' And in that day I accordingly disdained to supplicate them, on account of the fear of God. But in very deed I hoped of them that they would come into the faith of Jesus Christ, because they were heathen; and on account of this I clave to them. And we sailed immediately.

After three days we reached land, and for twenty-eight days we made our journey through a desert, and food failed them, and hunger prevailed over them. And one day the captain began to say to me, 'What, Christian, do you say? Thy God is great and almighty, why, therefore, canst thou not pray for us, for we are perishing with hunger? For it will be a difficult matter for us ever again to see any human being.' But I said to them plainly, 'Turn with faith to the Lord my God, to whom nothing is impossible, that He may send food this day for us in your path, even till you are satisfied, for it abounds everywhere with Him.' And God assisting, it so came to pass. Behold, a herd of swine appeared in the path before our eyes, and (my companions) killed many of them, and remained there two nights, much refreshed. And their dogs were filled, for many of them had been left exhausted along the way. And after that, they gave the greatest thanks to God, and I was honoured in their eyes.

From that day forth they had food in abundance. They also found wild honey, and offered me a part of it. And one of them said, 'This has been offered in sacrifice; Thanks to God!' I consequently tasted none of it. But the same night while I was sleeping, and Satan greatly tempted me, in a way which I shall remember as long as I am in this body, for he fell upon me like a huge rock, and there remained no power in my limbs, save that it came to me, into my mind, that I should call out 'Helias.' And in that moment I saw the sun rise in the heaven; and while I was crying out 'Helias,' with all my might, behold the splendour of that sun fell upon me, and at once removed the weight from me. And I believe I was aided by Christ my Lord, and His spirit was then crying out for me, and I hope likewise that it will be thus in the days of my oppression, as the Lord says in the Gospel, 'It is not you that speak, but the Spirit of your Father, which speaketh in you.'

And again, not many years afterward, I was taken captive once more, and on the first night therefore I remained with them. But I heard a divine response saying to me, 'Two months thou shalt be with them,' which accordingly came to pass. On the sixtieth night the Lord delivered me out of their hands.

Even on our journey He provided for us food and fire, and dry weather every day, till on the fourteenth day we all arrived. As I stated before, we pursued our journey for twenty-eight days through the desert, and the very night on which we all arrived we had no food left.

And again, after a few years, I was in Britain with my parents, who received me as a son, and earnestly besought me that, not at least, after the many hardships I had endured, I would never leave them again. And there I saw, indeed, in the bosom of the night, a man coming as it were from Ireland, Victoricus by name, with innumerable letters, and he gave one of them to me. And I read the beginning of the letter containing 'The Voice of the Irish.' And while I was reading aloud the beginning of the letter, I myself thought indeed in my mind that I heard the voice of the those who were near the wood Foclut, which is close by the Western Sea, and they cried out thus as if with one voice, 'We entreat thee, holy youth, that thou come, and henceforth walk among us.' And I was deeply moved in heart, and could read no further, and so I awoke. Thanks be to God, that after very many years the Lord granted to them according to their cry!

And on another night, I know not, God knows, whether in me, or near me, (one) spoke most eloquently in words which I heard, and could not understand, except at the end of his speech, as follows, 'He who gave for thee His life, is He who speaks in thee,' and so I awoke full of joy. And again I saw him praying in me, and I was as it were within my body, and I heard that is, above the inner man, and there he prayed mightily with groanings. And meanwhile, I was stupefied and astonished, and pondered who it could be that was praying in me. But at the end of the prayer he spoke as if he were the Spirit. And so I awoke, and remembered that the Apostle says, 'The Spirit helps the infirmities of our prayers. For we know not what we should pray for as we ought; but the Spirit himself asketh for us with unspeakable groanings,' which cannot be expressed in words. And again, (he says) 'The Lord is our advocate, and prays for us.'

And when I was attacked by some of my seniors, who came and urged my sins against my laborious episcopate, so that on that day I was strongly driven to fall away, here and for ever. But the Lord spared a proselyte and stranger for His name's sake. He kindly and mightily aided me in this treading-under, because in the stain and disgrace I did not come out badly. I pray God that it be not reckoned to them as an occasion of sin. After thirty years they found me, and brought against me a word which I had confessed before I was a deacon.

Under anxiety, with a troubled mind, I told my most intimate friend what I had one day done in my boyhood, nay in one hour; because I was not then used to overcome. I know not, God knows, whether I was then fifteen years of age; and I did not believe in the living God from my infancy; but I remained in death and unbelief, until I was severely chastised; and in truth I have been humbled by hunger and nakedness, and that daily. On the other hand I did not of my own accord go to Ireland, until I was almost worn out. But this was rather good for me; for by this I was corrected by the Lord – and He fitted me that I should be to-day what formerly was far from me; that I should be filled with care, and be concerned for the salvation of others; since at that time I did not think even about myself.

Then in that day on which I was reproached for the things above-mentioned; on that night, I saw in a vision of the night, a writing against me, without honour. And at the same time I heard a response saying to me, 'We have seen with displeasure the face of the designate with his name stripped.' He did not say, 'You have seen with displeasure,' but 'We have seen with displeasure,' as if He therein included Himself, as He has said, 'He that toucheth you, is as he that toucheth the apple of mine eye.' Therefore I give thanks to Him who comforted me in all things, that He did not hinder me from the journey which I had resolved on, and also from the work which I had learned of Christ my Lord. But the more from that (time) I felt no little power, and my faith was approved before God and men.

But on this account I boldly assert that my conscience does not reprove me now or for the future. God is my witness that I have not lied in the statements I have made to you. But I am the more sorry for my very dear friend, to whom I trusted even my life, that we should have deserved to hear such a response. And I ascertained before that defence from several brethren that, when I was not present, nor in Britain, and with which I had nothing to do – even he in my absence made a defence for me. Even he had said to me with his own mouth, 'Behold, thou art to be promoted to the rank of bishop,' although I was not worthy of it. But whence then did it occur to him afterwards that before all, good and bad, he should publicly put discredit on me, although he had before of his own accord gladly conceded (that honour to me)? But the Lord who is greater than all – I have said enough.

But however, I ought not to hide the gift of God which he bestowed upon us in the land of my captivity. For then I earnestly sought him, and there I found him, and he preserved me from all iniquities, so I believe, because of His Spirit, 'that dwelleth in (me),' which has wrought in me again boldly even to this day. But God knows, if a man had spoken this to me, I might have been silent for the love of Christ.

Wherefore, I give unwearied thanks to my God, who has kept me faithful in the day of my temptation; so that I may confidently offer to Him to-day my soul, – to Christ my Lord – as a sacrifice, 'a living victim'; Who saved me from all my difficulties, so that I may say: 'Who am I, Lord?' and what is my vocation, that to me Thou hast co-operated by such divine grace with me! So that to-day I can constantly rejoice among the Gentiles and magnify Thy name wherever I may be, not only in prosperity, but also in distresses; that whatever may happen to me whether good or evil, I ought to receive it equally and always to give thanks to God, who has shown me that I should believe in Him, the indubitable one, without ceasing, and that He will hear me; and that I, though ignorant, may in these last days attempt to approach His work, so pious and so wonderful, that I may imitate some of those of whom the Lord of old predicted (that they) should preach His Gospel, 'for a testimony to all nations' before the end of the world. Which, therefore, has been so fulfilled, as we have seen. Behold, we are witnesses that the Gospel has been preached everywhere, in places where there is no man beyond.

It would be long to relate all my labour, in details or even in part. Briefly, I may tell how the omnipotent God often delivered me from slavery, and from twelve dangers by which my life was imperilled, besides many snares, and things which I cannot express in words, neither would I give trouble to my readers. But there is God the author (of all), who knew all things before they came to pass, as He does me His poor pupil.

So however, the divine response very frequently admonished me (to consider) whence (came) this wisdom which was not in me, I who neither knew the number of my days, nor was acquainted with God? Whence (came) to me afterwards the gift so great, so beneficial, to know God, or to love Him, that I should leave country and parents? And many gifts were offered to me with weeping and tears. And, moreover, I offended against my wish certain of my seniors. But God overruling, I by no means consented or complied with them. It was not my grace, but God who conquered in me, and resisted them all; so that I came to the Irish peoples, to preach the Gospel, and to suffer insults from unbelievers; that I should listen to reproach about my wandering, and (endure) many persecutions, even to chains; and that I should give up my noble birth for the benefit of others.

And if I be worthy, I am ready to lay down my life unhesitatingly, and most gladly for His name; and there I wish to spend it, even till death, if the Lord permit.

For I am greatly a debtor to the God who has bestowed on me such grace, that many people through me should be born again to God, and that everywhere clergy should be ordained for a people newly come to the faith, whom the Lord took from the ends of the earth, as He had promised of old by His prophets. 'As our fathers falsely made idols, and there is no profit in them, to thee the Gentiles will come and say.' And again: 'I have set thee to be the light of the Gentiles, that thou mayest be for salvation unto the utmost part of the earth.' And there I am willing to wait the promise of Him who never fails, as He promises in the

Gospel: 'They shall come from the east and the west, and shall sit down with Abraham, and Isaac, and Jacob'; so we believe that believers shall come from all the world.

Therefore, it becomes us to fish well and diligently, as the Lord premonishes and teaches, saying: 'Come ye after me, and I will make you fishers of men.' And again he says by the prophets: 'Behold I send many fishers and hunters, saith the Lord.' Therefore it is very necessary to spread our nets, so that a copious multitude and crowd may be taken for God, and that everywhere there may be clergy who shall baptize and exhort a people so needy and desiring, as the Lord admonishes and teaches in the Gospel, saying: 'Going, therefore, teach ye all nations, baptizing them in the name of the Father, and of the Son, and of the Holy Spirit ... even to the end of the age.' And again: 'Going, therefore, into the whole world, preach the Gospel to every creature. He that believeth and is baptized, shall be saved, but he that believeth not shall be condemned.' And again: 'This Gospel of the kingdom shall be preached in the whole world, for a testimony to all nations and then shall consummation come. And also the Lord foretelling by the prophet, says: 'And it shall be in the last days, saith the Lord, I will pour out of my Spirit upon all flesh, and your sons and your daughters shall prophesy, and your sons shall see visions, and your old men shall dream dreams. And upon my servants indeed and upon my handmaids I will pour out in those days of my Spirit, and they shall prophesy.' And Osee says: 'I will call that which was not my people my people ... and her who had not obtained mercy, and it shall be in the place where it was said, you are not my people, there they shall be called the sons of the living God.'

Whence, then, has it come to pass that in Ireland they who never had any knowledge, and until now have only worshipped idols and unclean things, have lately become a people of the Lord, and are called the sons of God? Sons of the Scots and daughters of the chieftains are seen to be monks and virgins of

Christ. And there was even one blessed Scottic maiden, nobly-born, very beautiful, of adult age, whom I baptized. And after a few days she came to us for a reason, and intimated to us that she had received a response from a messenger of God, and he advised her that she should be a virgin of Christ, and that she should draw near to God. Thanks be to God! On the sixth day after that, she most excellently and eagerly seized on that which also all the virgins of God do; not with the will of their fathers – but they suffer persecution, and false reproaches from their parents; and the number increases notwithstanding; and of our own race who were born there, (there are those), we know not the number, besides chaste widows. But those who are detained in slavery especially suffer; in spite of terrors and threats they assiduously persevere. But the Lord gave grace to many of my handmaids, for they zealously imitate Him, if but so much.

Wherefore, though I could wish to leave them, and had been most willingly prepared to proceed to Britain, as to my country and parents; and not that only, but even (to go) as far as Gaul, to visit the brethren and to see the face of the saints of my Lord. God knows that I greatly desired it. But I am 'bound in the Spirit,' who 'witnesseth to me,' that if I should do this, He would hold me guilty; and I fear to lose the labour which I have commenced; and not I, but Christ the Lord, who commanded me to come, and be with them for the rest of my life. If the Lord will, and if He will keep me from every evil way, that I may not sin before Him. But I hope (to do) that which I ought; but I trust not myself, so long as I am in this body of death, for strong is he who daily strives to subvert me from the faith, and from the chastity of religion (to myself), not feignedly, even to the end of my life, to Christ my Lord. But the flesh which is in enmity, always leads to death, that is, to unlawful desires to be unlawfully gratified. And I know in part that I have not led a perfect life, as other believers. But I confess to my Lord, and I blush before Him, because I lie not, from the time that I knew

Him in my youth the love of God and His fear have increased in me; and until now, by the favour of the Lord, 'I have kept the faith.'

Let him who will laugh and insult, I will not be silent, nor will I hide the signs and wonders which were ministered to me by the Lord many years before they came to pass, as He who knew all things even before the world began.

But hence I ought to give thanks without ceasing to God, who, often pardoned my ignorance – my negligence out of place, not in one instance only – so that He was not fiercely angry with me, as being one who was permitted to be His helper. And yet I did not immediately yield to what was pointed out to me, and (to) what the Spirit suggested. And the Lord had pity on me among thousands of thousands, because He saw in me that I was ready, but that in my case for these (reasons) I knew not what to do about my position; because many were hindering this mission, and already were talking among themselves, and saying behind my back, 'Why does that fellow put himself into danger among enemies who know not God?' Not (as though they spoke) for the sake of malice, but because it was not a wise thing in their opinion, as I myself also testify, on account of my defect in learning. And I did not readily recognize the grace that was then in me; but now I know what I ought to have known before.

Now, therefore, I have related simply, to my brethren and fellow-servants who have believed me, (the reason) why I have preached and do preach, in order to strengthen and confirm your faith. Would that you might aim at greater, and perform mightier things! This will be my glory, because 'a wise son is the glory of a father.'

You know, and God also, how I have conducted myself among you from my youth, both in the faith of the truth, and in sincerity of heart. Even in the case of those nations among whom I dwell, I have always kept faith with them and I will keep it. God knows I have over-reached none of them; neither do I think of it, (that is, of acting thus) on account of God and his Church, lest I should excite persecution against them and us all, and lest through me the name of the Lord should be blasphemed; because it is written, 'Woe to the man through whom the name of the Lord is blasphemed.' For though I am unskilful in names, yet I have endeavoured in some respects to serve even my Christian brethren, and the virgins of Christ, and religious women, who have given to me small voluntary gifts, and have cast off some of their ornaments upon the altar; and I returned these to them, although they were offended with me because I did so. But I (did it) for the hope of eternal life, in order to keep myself prudently in everything, so that the unbelieving may not catch me on any pretext; or in respect to my ministering service, even in the smallest point, I might give the unbelievers an occasion to defame or depreciate it.

But perhaps, since I have baptized so many thousand men, I may have accepted half a screpall from some of them? Tell it to me and I will restore it to you. Or when the Lord ordained everywhere clergy, through my humble ministry, I dispensed the rite gratuitously. If I asked of any of them even the price of my shoe, tell it against me and I will restore you more. I spent for you, that they might receive me; and among you, and everywhere, I travelled for your sake, amid many perils, and even to remote places, where there was no one beyond, and where no one else had ever penetrated – to baptize or ordain clergy, or to confirm the people. The Lord granting it, I diligently and most cheerfully, for your salvation, defrayed all things. During this time I gave presents to the kings; besides which I gave pay to their sons who escorted me; and nevertheless they seized me together with my companions, and on that day they eagerly desired to kill me; but the time had not yet come. And they seized everything that was with us, and they also bound myself with iron. And on the fourteenth day the Lord set me free from their power; and whatever was ours was restored to us, for God's sake, and the attached friends whom we had before provided.

But you know how much I paid to those who acted as judges throughout all the regions which I more frequently visited. For I think that I distributed among them not less than the hire of fifteen men; that you might enjoy me, and I always enjoy you in the Lord. I do not regret it, nor is it enough for me – I still 'spend, and will spend for your souls.' God is mighty, and may He grant to me that in future I may spend myself for your souls. Behold, 'I call God to witness upon my soul that I lie not'; neither that you may have occasion, nor because I hope for honour from any of you. Sufficient to me is honour which is not belied. But I see that now I am exalted by the Lord above measure in the present age; and I was not worthy, nor deserving that He should aid me in this; since I know that poverty and calamity suit me better than riches and luxuries. But Christ the Lord was poor for us.

But I, poor and miserable, even if I wished for riches, yet have them not, 'neither do I judge my own self;' because I daily expect either murder, or to be circumvented, or to be reduced to slavery, or mishap of some kind. But 'I fear none of these things,' on account of the promises of the heavens; for I have cast myself into the hands of the Omnipotent God, because he rules everywhere, as saith the prophet, 'Cast thy thought on the Lord and he will sustain thee.'

Behold now, I commend my soul to my most faithful God, whose embassage I discharge in my ignoble condition, because indeed He does not accept the person, and He chose me to this office, that I might be one of the least of his ministers. But 'what shall I render Him for all the things that He hath rendered to me?' But what shall I say, or what shall I promise to my Lord? Because I see nothing, unless He had given it to me, but He searches 'the heart and reins'; because I desire enough and too much, and am prepared that He should give me 'to drink of His cup' as He has granted to others that love Him.

Wherefore may it never happen to me from my Lord, to lose my people, (people) whom He has gained in the utmost parts of the earth. I pray God that He may give me perseverance, and count me worthy to render faithful witness to Him, even till my departure, on account of my God. And if I have ever imitated anything good on account of my God, whom I love, I pray Him to grant me, that with those proselytes and captives, I may pour out my blood for His name's sake, even although, I myself may even be deprived of burial, and my corpse most miserably be torn limb from limb by dogs, or by wild beasts, or that the fowls of heaven should devour it. I believe most certainly that if this should happen to me, I shall have gained both soul and body. Because without any doubt we shall rise in that day in the brightness of the sun, that is, in the glory of Jesus Christ, our Redeemer, as sons of God, joint-heirs with Christ, and 'conformable to His image;' for of Him, and through Him, and in Him' we shall reign.

For that sun which we behold, at God's command, rises daily for us – but it shall never reign, nor shall its splendour continue, but all even that worship it, miserable beings, shall wretchedly come to punishment. But we who believe in, and adore the true sun, Christ, who will never perish, neither shall he 'who does His will,' – but 'shall continue forever' – who reigns with God the Father Almighty, and with the Holy Spirit, before the ages, and now, and through all the ages of ages. Amen.

Behold, I will, again and again, declare briefly the words of my Confession. I testify in truth, and in joy of heart, before God and His holy angels, that I never had any reason, except the gospel and its promises, for ever returning to that people from whom I had formerly escaped with difficulty.

But I beg of those who believe and fear God, whoever shall deign to look into, or receive this writing, which Patrick the sinner, unlearned indeed, has written in Ireland, that no one may ever say, if I have done or demonstrated anything, however little, that it was my ignorance (which did it). But judge ye, and let it be most truly believed, that it has been the gift of God. And this is my Confession before I die.

Translated by Rev. George Thomas Stokes
   and Rev. Charles H.H. Wright
The Writings of St Patrick the Apostle of Ireland, 1887

Saint Patrick's Epistle to Coroticus

I Patrick, a sinner and unlearned, have been appointed a bishop in Ireland, and I accept from God what I am. I dwell amongst barbarians as a proselyte and a fugitive for the love of God. He will testify that it is so. It is not my wish to pour forth so many harsh and severe things; but I am forced by zeal for God and the truth of Christ, who raised me up for my neighbors and sons, for whom I have forsaken my country and parents, and would give up even my life itself, if I were worthy. I have vowed to my God to teach these people, though I should be despised by them, to whom I have written with my own hand to be given to the soldiers to be sent to Coroticus – I do not say to my fellow-citizens, nor to the fellow-citizens of pious Romans, but to the fellow-citizens of the devil, through their evil deeds and hostile practices. They live in death, companions of the apostate Scots and Picts, bloodthirsty men, ever ready to redden themselves with the blood of innocent Christians, numbers of whom I have begotten to God and confirmed in Christ.

On the day following that in which they were clothed in white and received the chrism of neophytes, they were cruelly cut up and slain with the sword by the above mentioned; and I sent a letter by a holy priest, whom I have taught from his infancy, with some clerics, begging that they would restore some of the plunder or the baptized captives, but they laughed at them. Therefore, I know not whether I should grieve most for those who were slain, or for those whom the devil insnared into the eternal pains of hell, where they will be chained liked him. For whoever commits sin is the slave of sin, and is called the son of the devil.

Wherefore, let every man know who fears God that they are estranged from me, and from Christ my God, whose ambassador I am; these patricides, fratricides, and ravening wolves, who devour the people of the Lord as if they were bread; as it is said: 'The wicked have dissipated thy law;' wherein in these latter times Ireland has been well and prosperously planted and instructed. Thanks be to God, I usurp nothing; I share with these whom He hath called and predestinated to preach the Gospel in much persecution, even to the ends of the earth. But the enemy hath acted invidiously towards me through the tyrant Coroticus, who fears neither God, nor His priests, whom He hath chosen, and committed to them the high, divine power, 'Whomsoever they shall bind on earth shall be bound in heaven.'

I beseech you, therefore, who are the holy ones of God and humble of heart, that you will not be flattered by them, and that you will neither eat nor drink with them, nor receive their alms, until they do penance with many tears and liberate the servants of God and the baptized handmaids of Christ, for whom he was crucified and died. *He that offereth sacrifice of the goods of the poor, is as one that sacrificeth the son in the presence of the father.* 'Riches, he saith, which the unjust accumulate, shall be vomited forth from his belly, the angel of death shall drag him away, he shall be punished with the fury of dragons, the tongue of the adder shall slay him, inextinguishable fire shall consume him.' Hence, 'Woe to those who fill themselves with things which are not their own.' And *what doth it profit a man if he gain the whole world and suffer the loss of his soul?* It were too long to discuss one by one, or to select from the law, testimonies against such cupidity. Avarice is a mortal sin. 'Thou shalt not covet thy neighbor's goods.' 'Thou shalt not kill.' The homicide cannot dwell with Christ. *He who hateth his brother is a murderer,* and *he who loveth not his brother abideth in death.* How much more guilty is he who hath defiled his hands with the blood of the sons of God, whom He hath recently acquired in the ends of the earth by our humble exhortations!

Did I come to Ireland according to God or according to the flesh? Who compelled me, I was led by the Spirit, that I should see my relatives no more? Have I not a pious mercy towards that nation which formerly took me captive? According to the flesh I am of noble birth, my father being a Decurio. I do not regret or blush for having bartered my nobility for the good of others. I am a servant in Christ unto a foreign people, for the ineffable glory of eternal life, which is in Christ Jesus my Lord: though my own people do not acknowledge me: *A prophet is without honor in his own country.* Are we not from one stock, and have we not one God for our Father? As He has said: *He that is not with me is against me, and he that gathereth not with me scattereth.* Is it not agreed that one pulleth down and another buildeth? I seek not my own.

Not to me be praise, but to God, who hath put into my heart this desire, that I should be one of the hunters and fishers, whom, of old, God hath announced should appear in the last days. I am reviled – what shall I do, O Lord? I am greatly despised. Lo! thy sheep are around me, and plundered by the above-mentioned robbers, aided by the soldiers of Coroticus: the betrayers of Christians into the hands of the Picts and Scots are far from the charity of God. Ravening wolves have scattered the flock of the Lord, which, with the greatest diligence, was increasing in Ireland; the sons of the Irish, and the daughters of kings, who are too many to enumerate. Therefore, the oppression of the great is not pleasing to thee now, and never shall be.

Who of the saints would not dread to share in the feasts or amusements of such persons? They fill their houses with the spoils of the Christian dead, they live by rapine, they know not the poison, the deadly food which they present to their friends and children: as Eve did not understand that she offered death to her husband, so are all those who work evil; they labor to work out death and eternal punishment.

It is the custom of the Christians of Rome and Gaul to send holy men to the Franks and other nations, with many thousand solidi, to redeem baptized captives. You, who slay them, and sell them to foreign nations ignorant of God, deliver the members of Christ, as it were, into a den of wolves. What hope have you in God? Whoever agrees with you, or commands you? God will judge him. I know not what I can say, or what I can speak more of the departed sons of God slain cruelly by the sword. It is written: *Weep with them that weep.* And again: *If one member suffers anything, all the members suffer with it.* Therefore, the Church laments and bewails her sons and daughters, not slain by the sword, but sent away to distant countries, where sin is more shameless and abounds. There free-born Christian men are sold and enslaved amongst the wicked, abandoned, and apostate Picts.

Therefore, I cry out with grief and sorrow. O beautiful and well beloved brethren and children, whom I have brought forth in Christ in such multitudes, what shall I do for you? I am not worthy before God or man to come to your assistance. The wicked have prevailed over us. We have become outcasts. It would seem that they do not think we have one baptism and one Father, God. They think it an indignity that we have been born in Ireland: as He said: 'Have ye not one God? – why do ye each forsake his neighbor?' Therefore, I grieve for you, I grieve, O my beloved ones. But, on the other hand, I congratulate myself I have not labored for nothing – my journey has not been in vain. This horrible and amazing crime has been permitted to take place. Thanks be to God, ye who have believed and have been baptized have gone from earth to paradise. Certainly ye have begun to migrate where there is no night, nor death, nor sorrow, but ye shall exult, like young bulls loosed from their bonds, and tread down the wicked under your feet as dust.

Truly you shall reign with the apostles and prophets and martyrs, and obtain the eternal kingdom, as He hath testified, saying: *They shall come from the east and the west, and shall sit down with Abraham and Isaac and Jacob, in the kingdom of heaven.* Without are dogs, and sorcerers, and murderers, and liars, and perjurers, and they shall have their part in the everlasting lake of fire. Nor does the Apostle say without reason: 'If the just are scarcely saved, where shall the sinner, the impious, and the transgressor of the law appear?' Where will Coroticus and his wicked rebels against Christ find themselves, when they shall see rewards distributed amongst the baptized women? What will he think of his miserable kingdom, which shall pass away in a moment, like clouds or smoke, which are dispersed by the wind? So shall deceitful sinners perish before the face of the Lord, and the just shall feast with great confidence with Christ, and judge the nations, and rule over the unjust kings, for ever and ever. Amen.

I testify before God and His angels that it shall be so, as He hath intimated to my ignorance. These are not my words that I have set forth in Latin, but those of God and the prophets and apostles, who never lied: *He that believeth shall be saved, but he that believeth not shall be condemned.*

God hath said it. I entreat whosoever is a servant of God, that he be a willing bearer of this letter, that he be not drawn aside by any one, but that he shall see it read before all the people in the presence of Coroticus himself, that, if God inspire them, they may some time return to God, and repent, though late; that they may liberate the baptized captives, and repent for their homicides of the Lord's brethren; so that they may deserve of God to live and to be whole here and hereafter. The peace of the Father, and of the Son, and of the Holy Ghost. Amen.

Translated by M.F. Cusack
The Life of St. Patrick, Apostle of Ireland, 1871

Dicta Patricii: Sayings of Patrick

I had the fear of God as the guide of my journey through Gaul and Italy and, moreover, in the islands which are in the Tyrrhene Sea.

Ye departed from the world to Paradise. Thanks be to God.

Church of the Scots! nay, of the Romans! In order that ye be Christians as well as Romans ye must chant in your churches at every hour of prayer that glorious word, *Kyrie eleison, Christe eleison*. Let every church that follows me chant *Kyrie eleison, Christe eleison*.

Thanks be to God.

from the *Book of Armagh*
Translated by Newport J.D. White
St Patrick: His Writings and Life, 1920

St. Patrick's Breastplate.

Bind This day To me forever,
By power of faith, Christ's incarnation;
His baptism in Jordan river;
His death on Cross for my salvation;
His bursting from the spiced tomb;
His riding up the Heavenly way;
His coming at the day of doom;
I bind unto myself today.
Cuala Press.

Cuala Press, Dublin

Faeth Fiadha: The Breastplate of Saint Patrick

Patrick composed this hymn of Loegaire Meic Neill. It was made to shield him and his monks from deadly enemies who were ambushing the clerics.

And here is faith's trunk armour, to guard the body and soul from demons, desires and demented men. Devils will not fly in the face of him who recites it every day with his entire mind on God. It will protect him against poisons and jealousies, cherish him from a terrible end and armour his soul after death.

Patrick chanted it, travelling to Tara with the seed of faith, while Loegaire harassed his road. Passing through ambushes, he and his brethren had the look of wild deer; a fawn (called *Benen*) would trail behind them.

It is called The Deer's Cry.

TODAY I PUT ON
a terrible power,
   the invoked Trinity,
faith in the triple
abasement to the one
Macrocosm-Maker.

TODAY I PUT ON
the power of Christ
born, baptised
hanged, buried,
re-arisen, up-gathered,
due with final verdicts.

TODAY I PUT ON
power of Cherubim's love
assent of angels
administration of archangels

THE BREASTPLATE
OF SAINT PATRICK

Gerrit Van Gelderen

upsurge of desire for my prize
intercession of patriarchs
promises of prophets
guide-words of apostles
childlikeness of God's daughters
acts of proper men.

TODAY I PUT ON
the sinews of the sky
suns' flames
moon-shimmerings
fires' astonishment
the strike of lightning
forces of the wind
ocean's fissure
ground that will not give
solid rock.

TODAY I PUT ON
God's strength to steer me
God's power to pillar me
God's brain to guide me

God's eye to warn me
God's ear to listen for me
God's word to move my tongue
God's hand to guard me
God's track to meet my coming
God's shield to shelter me
God's millions to secure me from
    devils' traps
    vices' delights
    flaws of the flesh
    all-intent of enemies
        distant and close
        singly, in hosts.

I CALL THESE POWERS
    to take my part
against every warped, implacable power
    that would stray my soul and body
against incantations of false prophets
against dark enactments of the gentiles
against the wrong laws of heretics
against sterility of idolatry
against spells of women, smiths and druids
against every inkling of evil in man's body
                and soul.

I CALL CHRIST TODAY
    to guard me from
    poison, burning
    drowning, injury
that all rewards may be my due
Christ by me, Christ before me,
    Christ behind me
Christ within me, Christ beneath me,
    Christ above me

Christ on my left hand,
    Christ on my right
Christ in the breast of all who behold me
Christ on the tongues of all who talk of me
Christ in every eye that sees me
Christ in every ear that hears me.

TODAY I PUT ON
a terrible power, the invoked Trinity
faith in the triple
abasement to the one
Macrocosm-Maker.

DOMINI EST SALUS
DOMINI EST SALUS
DOMINI EST SALUS
SALUS TUA DOMINE,
SIT SEMPER NOBISCUM
AMEN

Faeth Fiadha: The Breastplate of Saint Patrick
Translated by Thomas Kinsella, 1957

McKee, Belfast

'St Patrick opening his Purgatory'
by C.J. Ciappori-Puche (1822–87)

3

PLACES OF PILGRIMAGE

Throughout Ireland there are numerous places that have a strong Patrician heritage and tradition. The number of churches and cathedrals that bear his name outweigh those of any other Irish saint. Devotion to the patron saint of Ireland has spread across Europe, and, as we shall see in chapter five, into the New World. It may, therefore, be surprising that the birthplace of the saint remains a matter of debate. The imprecise geographical accounts of his native home has led to various towns in Britain, northern France, and Spain, claiming the honour of being his birthplace.

In Ireland there is greater, though not unanimous, agreement on Patrician sites. Slemish is the place where Patrick dwelt for six years as the slave of Milchu; Armagh was founded by Patrick; he began his mission in Saul, County Down; he spent nights reciting the psalms in wet conditions at nearby Struell Wells; he performed miracles at Tara and Cashel; he journeyed into Leinster and Munster; he spent forty days fasting on Croagh Patrick and he did penance on Lough Derg. Downpatrick is the place of his burial, his bones – with those of Brigid and Colmcille – rescued and re-interred beside the Cathedral of Down by the Norman ruler of Dalriada, John de Courcy. Many towns and villages throughout Ireland revere the tradition of Patrick's mission in their locality. The Wood of Foclut is more problematic, however, being sited by some in County Mayo, in County Antrim – even in Brittany, in northern France.

Continental towns associated with Patrick, from Muirchú's and Jocelin's *Life of Saint Patrick*, include Auxerre, Tours and Rome. The cult of Patrick was carried into Europe by Irish monks and clerics who founded churches in Italy, Spain, France and Germany; and veneration of the saint remains part of religious tradition in such far-flung places as Drackenstein in Germany, Rouen in France, Bergamo in Italy, and Santiago and Salamanca in Spain.

Today, the legacy of the boy from Roman Britain, who brought Christianity to the pagan Irish, is celebrated in an increasingly secular world. The places of his fifth-century mission continue to be places of pilgrimage for the faithful and for the seekers after the spiritual.

Diocese of Down and Dromore

'St Patrick on Slemish', Down Cathedral, Downpatrick

Where, then, was St. Patrick born?

Where, then, was St. Patrick born? To this query there have been very many conflicting replies. Ireland itself has claimed the honour. Scotland and France have each their vigorous champions. The claim of Ireland we may at once dismiss. It is founded on a passage in St. Patrick's Epistle to the British prince Coroticus, where he speaks of the contemptuous feeling cherished in the hearts of the Britons towards Irish-men,– a feeling which fourteen centuries have not sufficed to quite destroy. Listen to this early protest against a sentiment which has wrought untold mischief. 'The Church,' he says, 'weeps and wails over her sons and over her daughters, whom the sword has not yet slain, but who are exiled and carried away to far-off lands, where sin openly prevails and shamelessly abounds. There, Christian freemen are reduced to slavery, and that by the most unworthy, most infamous, and apostate Picts … The unrighteousness of the unrighteous hath prevailed over us. We are become as aliens. Perchance they do not believe that we have received one baptism, that we have one God our Father. With them it is a crime that we have been born in Hibernia; but it is said, have ye not one God? Why do ye wrong to one another?'

These words – 'with them it is a crime that we have been born in Hibernia' – constitute the whole foundation of Ireland's claim to have been the birthplace of St. Patrick. It is evident, however, that he is thereby merely identifying himself with his converts; while in other parts of his works he asserts in the clearest and most positive manner that he was not an Irishman by birth.

Some, again, have maintained the claim of Boulogne, others that of Dumbarton on the Clyde …

The opinion of critics seems now inclined to assign the honour to Dumbarton, which in ancient times was called Alcluith, and formed the western termination of the great Roman wall, extending from the Forth to the Clyde, constructed by Agricola about the year 80, and renewed under Antoninus Pius, to protect Northern Britain from the attacks of the savage Highlanders. To this view, as I have hinted above, the greater number of modern critics seem inclined, though, like all such questions, there is much to be said on the other side, and if one be inclined to argue, it will be impossible to demonstrate the erroneous character of his views. All the circumstances, however, tend to confirm the claim of Dumbarton. Its local position is in its favour. The 'finds' of Roman coins upon the opposite Antrim coast, dating in such quantities from St. Patrick's day, sustain it, while again another circumstance corroborates it. Mark how this was. St. Patrick tells us, in the Epistle to Coroticus, that he was of noble birth; that his father was a decurion, a member of the local town council – an institution which prevailed as a useful species of local government in all colonies and municipalities throughout the wide domains of Rome, from farthest East to the shores of the North Atlantic Ocean. Let me dwell upon this point, which is rather obscure; for, indeed, with all our classical studies, there is no subject over which a thicker darkness prevails among English students than the methods of government and administration used by the Roman Empire. Of late years there have come to light in Spain some very curious documents which illustrate these methods. In pursuing the course of some ancient Roman mines, the explorers came across tablets containing laws made to regulate imperial mining colonies during the first and second centuries of our era. These laws descend to the minutest particulars, proving the comprehensiveness and perfection of Roman legislation and of the Roman civil service. Among other regulations we find that town councils or local senates, composed of decurions, were appointed as soon as a few hundred persons were assembled together in a town or village. Decurions, therefore, must certainly have existed at Dumbarton at the close of the fourth century. Again, St. Patrick tells us he was carried captive with some thousands of his countrymen, whom God visited for their sins. Now, at the end of the fourth century Northern Britain was ravaged by Picts and Scots, and thousands were led captives, till the most famous generals of the empire, Theodosius and Stilicho, were sent to restore tranquillity to the desolated island.

St Patrick, in his writings, always speaks of Britain in the plural, denominating it Britanniæ, which was strictly accurate. Theodosius, after expelling the Irish and Pictish foe, organised Northern Britain into a separate province, called Valentia, the names of the other provinces being Britannia Prima, Britannia Secunda, Maxima Cæsariensis, and Flavia Cæsariensis. His original name, too, was Succath, a Celtic name, such as naturally would find place in a population living in the midst of Celts, even if his family was not originally Celtic, as probably was the case, though at the same time conforming themselves as the Britons largely did, to the institutions, language, religion and civilisation of Rome.

So much as to the place of his birth.

George T. Stokes
Ireland and the Celtic Church, 1886

Rediscovering Patrice

As we drove through old wrought-iron gates along a tree-lined avenue towards the front entrance of the hotel there was a moment of sudden anxiety and disappointment. We expect a French château to be luxurious, extravagant and well kept but this one, at first sight, seemed neglected. First impressions are notoriously unreliable. I had travelled to France with a friend to research some of the sacred sites associated with the Celtic

Tradition in Brittany, in preparation for a pilgrimage planned for the following year.

The hotel – the Château de Bonaban, Brittany – had been booked online at the last minute, simply to provide a break from work and celebrate a jubilee birthday. All the tower rooms at the château have high ceilings and spectacular views of the grounds and surrounding forest. I noticed a coat of arms at the top of a sheet of headed note paper which had been left on the table. Written in French with an English translation, it provided basic information for guests about the château's history and local significance. What I read next came as a complete and total surprise that would change my image and understanding of St Patrick forever.

> The first castle or rather fortress that was built here dates from the Roman period, during the fourth century. At that time, this place was called Bonavenna (or Bonabes) de Tiberio. It belonged to a Scottish prince, Calpurnius, who had come here to avoid Saxon forces who were invading Britain ... One night, Irish pirates arrived in nearby Cancale. They spread through the Wood of Quokelunde, which stretched under Gouesnière-Bonaban as far as Plerguèr. Armed with pikes and axes, they slaughtered the prince and all his family. His property was looted and the castle burned to the ground ... Only his young son, Patrice, survived from this slaughter. He was taken captive to Ireland. There he looked after sheep and learned the language of the country of which he became the oracle and the disciple.

I have read a lot of books about the Irish saints and have visited many of the ancient, sacred sites associated with St. Patrick in Ireland, but before arriving at this hotel I had no idea whatsoever that Patrick had any connections with Brittany. I had to read this information again several times to process the enormity of what was being said, as the significance of these claims began to sink in. Could this really be the place where St Patrick once lived, before he was taken captive and sold as a slave in Ireland?

Marcus Losack
Rediscovering Saint Patrick: A New Theory of Origins, 2013

Slemish in the Days of St. Patrick

When visiting Slemish one naturally endeavours to visualise the mountain and the surrounding district as it was when St. Patrick worked there as a slave. Doubtless, the mountain itself was then much the same as it is today. Here and there rocks, boulders, and banks of soil may have become dislodged and have tumbled down; but since this is a rare enough occurrence we are safe in saying that, all in all, Slemish is today what it was in St. Patrick's day. When he walked on these slopes he saw, as we do now, furze bushes, wild roses, briars, willow trees, abundant growths of fuchsia, and hazel trees; for all these are indigenous to the locality. Hazel trees flourish in the soil here: the farmers of the district say that hazel trees spring up in any land left untilled.

When working in the bog – especially in the damp hollows – on the eastern side of Slemish, local farmers often come upon strong, thick roots of trees buried in the turf. To cut and lever out these tenacious roots a long-handled axe with a thick narrow head of iron is used. In the farmyard of Mr. Mills, a Protestant farmer at Slemish, I saw a pile of these roots. Some of them were as thick as the trunk of a fifty-year-old tree. These roots are full of resin. They are fir or pine. So plentiful are these roots in the area around Slemish that it is certain the lower slopes of the mountain were once well-wooded with these trees.

In his *Confession* Patrick says: 'After I came to Ireland, tending flocks was my daily occupation.' The Latin word he uses for 'flocks' is '*pecora*', which may mean flocks of sheep, herds of pigs, or droves of cattle. Perhaps he had to tend all these. The farmers and shepherds of Slemish say that no man in his senses would bring pigs or cattle on to the mountain itself: in many places the sides of Slemish are so steep that these animals would certainly fall and be killed. These experienced men firmly assert that Patrick must have herded swine and cattle on the lower slopes and watched over sheep on the mountain itself. Dr. MacNeill tells us it was customary in ancient Ireland to keep large herds of swine in the forests. This is most probably what happened at Slemish in Patrick's time.

Slemish is an ideal mountain for sheep: there is plenty of good, sweet picking on it, shelter at all times from wind and rain, a slight breeze in summer which keeps flies from tormenting the sheep; and because of the hard, rocky ground there has never been in living memory a case of foot-rot among the sheep. Patrick alone could never have done all the work with his flocks. To give one example of how he needed help: at lambing time today it takes five men with dogs to bring down the sheep from Slemish: two men work their way along the side slopes and three others clear the summit.

When bringing down the sheep from the mountain, or pigs from the wooded slopes, the obvious way of descent is by the easy slopes on the north-eastern side. No other way is as safe and secure as this. Where level ground is reached by this way of descent, in the farm land of Mr. Frank Magill, a Catholic farmer, you come upon the tumbled walls of at least three half-moon shaped enclosures, forty or fifty feet long at the diameter wall. Within these enclosures are a number of smaller ones. By rough calculation, one of these inner enclosures measures ten by fourteen feet. The local people call these enclosures St. Patrick's Pig 'Croos' or 'Crays' – I give the phonetic spelling. The original word for these is the Scottish 'cruive' or 'cruve', which means a pig-sty. Here in these cruives the young pigs of the herd were kept until they were able to go out to the mountain slopes and fend for themselves. The outer walls of these cruives appear to have been much higher than the inner walls. The stones forming them have, for the most part, fallen down. These stones are very large and are covered now with brown moss. Hazel trees and briar have grown thickly at the spot: if these were cleared away the exact size and structure of the cruives could easily be determined.

Slemish Mountain near Broughshane

Another interesting item concerning St. Patrick's life as a slave on Slemish was told to me by Mr. John Lecky, a Protestant farmer who has lived all his life at Slemish. He said that about sixty years ago, when he was a small boy, he went with his father on a fine day along the south-eastern side of Slemish. About thirty or forty feet up the mountain side they found a sheep caught in a deep cave. They extricated it safely. To prevent further harm to sheep they blocked up this cave, and also two others nearby, with stones. These caves are natural caves – 'not made by the hand of man' is Mr. Lecky's phrase; they are deep and their entrance is about three or four feet square.

For a moment let us recall St. Patrick's own words in the *Confession*:

After I came to Ireland tending flocks was my daily occupation, and constantly I used to pray in the daytime. Love of God and the fear of Him increased more and more, and faith grew and the spirit was moved so that in one day I would say as many as a hundred prayers, and at night nearly as many, while I was out in the woods and on the mountain side. Before daybreak I used to be roused to prayer, in snow, in frost, in rain.

Did Patrick, while out at night on the mountain side, find rest and shelter in these caves? As I have said earlier, in winter the cold winds of the north and the east bring snow and frost and hail to Slemish. The sheltered side of the mountain would then be this south-western side where the caves lie. Since they furnish excellent shelter, is it not likely that our saint, who knew the mountain so thoroughly, used these caves for shelter during those wild bitterly cold nights? With a bed of dry fern and bracken they could afford him better shelter than the overhanging ledges of rock on the mountain side.

During the year many Catholics out of love for St. Patrick visit Slemish. A number of them approach the mountain on its steep sides and find the ascent very difficult. In this article I have described the best mode of approach.

On St. Patrick's Day a considerable number of priests come with school-children. They climb the mountain easily and on the summit recite the Rosary and sing hymns in honour of our saint.

Slemish ought to be dear to us all. There St. Patrick spent six years; there he was 'greatly chastened and humbled in truth by hunger and nakedness', and there through his prayerful acceptance of his exile and sufferings he turned to God. On Slemish by God's grace he started his life-work among the Irish people by first giving himself to God. Tradition tells us he even taught Miliuc's children the way of Christ. And, moreover, as Dr. MacNeill says, 'the familiarity that St. Patrick acquired, during his captivity, with the language of Ireland fitted him providentially for his future mission'.

One point more in conclusion. The ownership of Slemish today is shared by two Catholics and four Protestants. The title of ownership is called rundale, that is, there is joint occupation of the land, each holder having several strips not contiguous. Apart from legal title, however, does not Slemish in a certain real sense form part of the priceless heritage of the Irish people?

D.M. Cummings, Clonard Monastery, Belfast
The Furrow, 1955

St. Patrick's Sojourn in Auxerre

But for the thirty years of his episcopacy from 418 to 448, Germanus, except for his two missions to Great Britain and the journey to Ravenna in the course of which he died, had resided habitually in the episcopal city. So if in actual fact Patrick did place himself for many years under Germanus's guidance, the island called *Aralanum*, or *Aralana*, where Tirechán declares Patrick to have spent thirty years, should not be sought in the Tyrrhenean sea but must necessarily be sought in the immediate vicinity of Auxerre where Germanus resided.

The reasoning which we follow here was already made by the author of the *Vita Tripartita*, which declares with great precision:

> *Autisiodorum nomen erat civitatis cuius S. Germanus erat superior et nobilis antistes; Aralanensis vocabatur insula in qua S. Patricius apud eum erudiebatur.*
>
> Auxerre was the name of the city in which Germanus was the head and noble bishop; Aralanensis the name of the island where St. Patrick was instructed at his feet.

Another version of the life of St. Patrick, the *Vita Secunda*, agrees with Bishop Ultan in ascribing to Patrick a thirty years' sojourn on the island (insula) but it emphasises that the thirty years were spent in the company of Germanus:

> *Pervenit ad Germanum in insula Aralanensi nomine, in qua docuit eum. Triginta tunc annos impleverat; triginta annis legit cum illo; sexaginta annis praedicavit in Hibernia.*
> He came to Germanus in the island called Aralanensis where he instructed him. Patrick was then thirty years old. For another thirty years he studied under him (Germanus). Then he preached for sixty years in Ireland.

The novitiate, preparing Patrick for his Irish apostolate, surely did not last thirty years; the chronology which proceeds in periods of thirty and sixty years ought to be considered imaginary and inspired by speculations on the perfection of the number three and its multiples. Even granted that Germanus was elected bishop of Auxerre in 418 and that Patrick left Auxerre in 432 never to return, one cannot see how Patrick, even if he was in Auxerre from the beginning of Germanus's episcopate in 418, could have been his disciple for more than fourteen years.

True, some historians reckon that Patrick came to Auxerre during the reign of the predecessor of Germanus, Amator, who may have reigned from 388 and who died on 1st May 418. But this opinion is based only on the narrative of Muirchú, another Irish biographer of the seventh century, who affirms that Patrick, after the death (432) of Palladius, the first bishop of the Irish, received episcopal consecration from a holy bishop, named Mathorex: "*episcopalem gradum a Mathorege sancto episcopo accepit*" (Book of Armagh, fo. 2v). Mathorex, however, is a Celtic name which has nothing in common with the Latin name, Amator. Furthermore as Amator died in 418, he cannot be identified with the Mathorex of 432 of whom, up to the present, we know nothing.

To conclude – Patrick lived in Auxerre only during the reign of Germanus, between 418 at the earliest and 432 ...

Though he ardently wished to undertake the evangelisation of Ireland, Patrick, the monk, in obedience to his superiors at Auxerre, had to bide his time and wait long years before he could realise his dream. In 431, Palladius, the same man who in 429 had brought instructions to Germanus from the Holy See concerning his mission to Great Britain, left Rome for Ireland. He had been consecrated bishop of the country by Pope Celestine. At Auxerre, he broke his journey to consult Germanus. Must not Patrick, impatiently tied to the banks of the Yonne, have regarded the happy traveller with envy?

The following year Patrick won from Germanus permission to go to Ireland to labour there as a simple priest under Bishop Palladius. But Germanus did not wish that his spiritual son should travel alone. He sent with him two companions with whom Patrick had been ordained: Auxilius and the Irishman Iserninus. He also sent the priest Segitius to supervise Patrick's conduct and to report back to him: *ut testem comitem haberet.*

When the four priests had received the blessing of Germanus, they set out along the Roman road, the road of Agrippa which, leaving Auxerre by the Roman bridge – the present Paul-Bert Bridge – runs to Troyes and ends at Boulogne-sur-Mer. They halted at a place called Eboria, Euboria or Ebmoria according to the different manuscripts. As far as I am concerned, I think this place should be sought on the Channel Coast of England. There the four travellers met Augustinus and Benedictus, companions of Palladius, who told them that Palladius had died after an apostolate of only a few months. It was then that Patrick went to the saintly bishop Mathorex, who lived near Eboria, and was consecrated bishop by him. As bishop, he resumed his journey to Ireland.

René Louis
Seanchas Ardmhacha: Journal of the Armagh Diocesan Society,
  1961/62

Patrick is consecrated by Celestinus in Rome

The Airchinnech that was in Rome at that time was Celestinus, the forty-second man from Peter. He sent Palladius, a high deacon, with twelve men, to instruct the Gaeidhel (for to the comarb of Peter belongs the instruction of Europe), in the same way as Barnabas went from Peter to instruct the Romans, etc.

When Palladius arrived in the territory of Leinster – *i.e.*, at InbherDea – Nathi, son of Garchu, opposed him, and expelled him. And Palladius baptized a few there, and founded three churches – viz., Cill-fine (in which he left his books, and the casket with the relics of Paul and Peter, and the tablet in which he used to write), and Tech-na-Roman, and Doinhnach-Airte, in which Silvester and Solonius are. On turning back afterwards, sickness seized him, in the country of the Cruithne, and he died of it.

When Patrick heard this thing, and knew that it was for him God designed the apostleship of Erinn, he went subsequently to Rome to receive grade; and it was Celestinus, Abbot of Rome, who read *grada* (orders, degrees) over him; Germanus and Amatho, King of the Romans, being present with them.

Anon.
The Tripartite Life of Saint Patrick
Translated by Whitley Stokes, 1887

Saul: The Place of Patrick's Landing

This year, 1932, will be memorable in Irish annals – the year of the celebration of two events of rare and supreme interest – the 31st International Eucharistic Congress, and the Fifteenth Centenary of the landing of St. Patrick on our shores.

The site of his landing has been located with accuracy. Before 1932 passes away there will stand in Saul, if our earnest hope is realised, a fitting memorial of that ever-to-be-remembered event in the very place where Patrick began – and where also he ended – his missionary labours.

On the slopes of Slemish, in the heart of the adjoining County of Antrim, he had already spent in the hard life of a slave six youthful years of penance, prayer, and privation – six years of preparation. Then he left Ireland, a fugitive slave, but was destined soon to return as its Apostle.

Commissioned by the Apostolic See, he came back to preach the Gospel to a race which has ever since kept its feet firmly fixed on the Rock of Peter. Homeless, he landed at Saul. At

Saul he found a home and friends. There, Dichu, the earliest of his converts, gave him that barn in which, for the first time on Irish soil, he offered the adorable Sacrifice of the Mass. As it was Patrick's first, doubtless it was his best beloved, Church. There his blessed work began. From Saul it spread over the Island till the children of the Gael, one and all, were brought within one Fold and under one Shepherd.

Thus to Saul belongs the pre-eminent honour of having been the cradle of the Faith in our land.

Saul was the place of all most dear to the heart of Patrick. Saul he chose for the beginning of his tireless Apostleship. To Saul – when his long day's work was done, and he had won the Irish from shore to shore for Christ, his Divine Master – he came back to die. In Saul were his

96

obsequies attended by bishops and chieftains from the remotest parts of Ireland. The Saint's place of burial is at Downpatrick – two miles west of Saul.

Anon.
Down and Connor Historical Society's Journal, 1931

Saul Church, Saul, County Down

Struell Wells

On the east-side of the Road, having passed *Ballee-Church*, and the mountain called *Slieve na-Grideal*, remarkable for a monument of antiquity at the top of it, we come to the celebrated *Wells of St. Patrick*, otherwise called *Struell-Wells*, from a town land of that name, whereon they spring; to which vast Throngs of Rich and Poor resort on *Mid-Summer-Eve*, and the *Friday* before *Lammas*, some in hopes of obtaining Health and others

The main building at Struell Wells, Downpatrick

to perform Penances enjoined them by the Popish Priests from the Water blessed by *St. Patrick*. They are four in Number, each covered with a vault of stone, and the Water is conveyed by subterraneous Aqueducts from one to the other; but the largest of these Vaults is the most celebrated, being in dimensions sixteen feet and a half by eleven, and is more particularly said to have received *St. Patrick*'s Benediction. In this they bathe the whole body, there being a commodious Chamber fitted up for dressing and undressing; and the Water of this Well may be raised to what height you please, by means of a Sluice. The other Wells are applied for washing particular Parts of the Body, as the Eyes, Head, Limbs etc. All these Vaults seem to be very Antient, and near one of them are the Ruins of a small Chappel, dedicated to *St. Patrick*. The Water of these Fountains are perfectly limpid and pleasant.

Walter Harris
The Ancient and Present State of the County of Down, 1744

St Patrick's Grave, *Graphic*, 1900

The Burial Place of St. Patrick

The year of St. Patrick's death has been fixed at 492. It took place at Saul, where, as already stated, he had founded his first church in Ireland. It was his wish to have been interred in Armagh, and after his death a controversy arose between the ecclesiastics of Armagh and Dundalethglass (the ancient ecclesiastical name of Downpatrick) as to where he should be interred. In order to settle the controversy, it was arranged that two untamed oxen should be yoked to the bier, and wherever they stopped, there the burial place was to be. The Annals add, 'They rested at Dundalethglass, the site of the present Cathedral of Down.' As in the case of his birth, several localities contend for the honour of his burial-place, but all claimants may be dismissed save those of Armagh and Downpatrick. As to the claim of Armagh, so far back as the year 802, the 'Book of Armagh' stated that he was buried in Downpatrick. The claims of Downpatrick are clearly and succinctly set forth by the late Dr. William Reeves, Bishop of Down, in a letter to the Hon. Sec. of the Cathedral Board. The Board were considering as to erecting a monument over the reputed grave in the old cemetery attached to the Cathedral, but before taking any decisive step they consulted Dr. Reeves (who was then Dean of Armagh, and whose reputation as an antiquarian is world-wide) as to whether the reputed spot was really the burial-place. The following is his reply:

April 16th, 1875

MY DEAR SIR, — I am strongly of the opinion that any attempt to localise to a certain spot the place of St. Patrick's burial is futile and absurd. That he was interred at Downpatrick, and there in consecrated ground, I truly believe, for it is an unbroken tradition of such antiquity that he who denies it may safely question the evidence for the Saint's existence at all. But to presume to fix any one grave in the churchyard, or to follow any one vulgar tradition, which must of modern origin, as to the actual spot is ridiculous. When we consider that in his case, as of all the eminent Saints of primitive times, the body was not long in the grave before the substantial remains, which were the skeleton, were disinterred and enshrined, and so removed from their resting-place, leaving to the grave but little honour, but to history the undeniable fact that he died and was buried in or near a certain church and that his reliques were for a time preserved there. Therefore the honour and lustre of St. Patrick's burial belongs not to an unknown patch of a few feet in the cemetery, but to the town, and more especially the ancient church of that town. In this case Downpatrick is the town, and the utmost limitation of place in that town is the Cathedral and its precincts. The Cathedral represents the primitive church of his day, and any memorial must be in connexion with that structure: but an attempt to specify the exact grave would be to render the monument presumptuous, and to throw discredit upon the whole procedure.

Yours faithfully,

WILLIAM REEVES

Edward Parkinson
Historical Sketch of the Cathedral of Down, 1904

Of the City of Ardmachia, and Twelve of its Citizens

Then Patrick founded, according to the direction of the angels, a city, fair in its site, its form, and its ambit, and when by the divine assistance it was completed, he brought to dwell therein twelve citizens, whom he had from all parts diligently and discreetly chosen: and these he instructed in the Catholic doctrines of the Christian faith. And he beautified the city with churches builded after a becoming and spiritual fashion; and for the observance of divine worship, for the government of souls, and for the instruction of the Catholic flock, he appointed therein clerical persons; and he instituted certain monasteries filled with monks, and others filled with nuns, and placed them under the regulations of all possible perfection. And in one of these monasteries was a certain brother, who would not take either food or drink before the hour appointed by the saint; and he perished of thirst; and Patrick beheld his soul ascending into heaven, and placed among the martyrs. And in the convent of the handmaidens of God, was a certain virgin, the daughter of a British king, with nine other holy damsels, who had come with her unto Saint Patrick, and of these, three in his presence went unto heaven. And in this city placed he an archiepiscopal cathedral; and determined in his mind that it should be the chief metropolis, and the mistress of all Hibernia; and that this his purpose might remain fixed and by posterity unaltered, he resolved to journey unto the apostolic seat, and confirm it with authentic privileges.

And the angel of the Lord appearing unto Patrick, approved the purpose of his journey, and showed him that the Pope would bestow and divide among many churches the relics of the Apostles Peter and Paul, and of many saints. And as carriages were haply then wanting unto him, the angels provided him with four chariots, as if sent from heaven, the which conveyed him and his people unto the sea-side. Then the glorified prelate Patrick; after that the urgency of his laborious preaching was finished, and the abundance of so many and so great miracles had converted the whole island, blessed and bade farewell to the several bishops and presbyters and other members of the church whom he had ordained: and with certain of his disciples, led by his angelic guide, he sailed toward Rome. Whither arriving, while in the presence of the supreme pontiff he declared the cause of his coming, supreme favor he found in his eyes; for, embracing and acknowledging him as the apostle of Hibernia, he decorated the saint with the pall, and appointing him his legate, by his authority confirmed whatsoever Patrick had done, appointed or disposed therein. And many parting presents, and precious gifts, which pertained unto the beauty, nay, unto the strength of the church, did the Pope bestow on him; where-among were certain relics of the Apostles Peter and Paul, and of Stephen the proto-martyr, and of many other martyrs; and moreover, gave he unto the saint a linen cloth, which was marked with the blood of our Lord the Saviour Jesus Christ. Gift excelling all other gifts! And with these most holy honors the saint being returned unto Hibernia, fortified therewith this metropolitan church of Ardmachia (unto the salvation of souls and the safety of the whole nation), and reposited them in a chest behind the great altar. And in that church even from the time of Saint Patrick the custom obtained that on the days of the Passover and of the Pentecost these relics should be thereout produced, and venerated in the presence of the people.

Jocelin
Life and Acts of Saint Patrick
Translated by Edmund L. Swift
The Most Ancient Lives of Saint Patrick, 1874

Patrick lights the Pascal Fire on Tara Hill

When the solemnity of Easter approached, Patrick considered that there was no place more suitable to celebrate the high solemnity of the year – *i.e.*, the Easter – than in Magh-Bregh, the place where the head of the idolatry and druidism of Erinn was – viz., in Temhair. They afterwards bade farewell to Dichu, son of Trichim, and put their vessels on the sea; and they proceeded until they anchored in Inbher-Colptha. They left their vessels in

Ruth Brandt

the Inbher, and went by land until they reached Ferta-fer-féc, and Patrick's tent was fixed in this place, and he cut the Easter fire. It happened, however, that this was the time in which the great festival of the Gentiles – *i.e.*, the *Fes of Tara* – was usually celebrated. The kings and princes and chieftains were wont to come to Laeghaire Mac Neill to Tara, to celebrate this festival. The druids and the magicians were also wont to come to prophesy to them. The fire of every hearth in Erinn was usually extinguished on that night, and it was commanded by the king that no fire should be lighted in Erinn before the fire of Tara, and neither gold nor silver would be accepted from any one who would light it, but he should suffer death for it. Patrick knew not this thing; and if he knew it, it would not prevent him.

As the people of Tara were thus, they saw the consecrated Easter fire at a distance which Patrick had lighted. It illuminated all Magh-Bregh. Then the king said: 'That is a violation of my prohibition and law; and do you ascertain who did it.' 'We see the fire,' said the druids, 'and we know the night in which it is made. If it is not extinguished before morning,' added they, 'it will never be extinguished. The man who lighted it will surpass the kings and princes, unless he is prevented.' When the king heard this thing, he was much infuriated. Then the king said: 'That is not how it shall be; but we will go,' said he, 'until we slay the man who lighted the fire.' His chariot and horses were yoked for the king, and they went, in the end of the night, to Ferta-fer-féc. 'You must take care,' said the druids, 'that you go not to the place where the fire was made, lest you worship the man who lighted it; but stay outside, and let him be called out to you, that he may know you to be a king, and himself a subject; and we will argue in your presence.' 'It is good counsel,' said the king, 'it shall be done as you say.' They proceeded afterwards until they unyoked their horses and chariots in front of the *Ferta*. Patrick was 'whispered' out to them; and it was commanded by them that no one should rise up before him, lest he should believe in him. Patrick rose and went out; and when he saw the chariots and horses unyoked, he sang the prophetic stanza:

Hi in curribus et hi in eorus (equis),
Nos autem, in nomine Domini Dei nostri ma.

They were then before him, and the rims of their shields against their chins; and none of them rose up before him, except one man alone, in whom was a figure from God – *i.e.*, Ere, son of Dega. He is the Bishop Ere who is [commemorated] in Slaine of Magh-Bregh to-day. Patrick blessed him, and he believed in God, and confessed the Catholic faith, and was baptized; and Patrick said to him: 'Your seat (*cathair*, chair or city) on earth shall be noble'; and Patrick's (*comarb*) successor is bound to bend the knee before his *comarb* in consideration of his submission.

Each then questioned the other – viz., Patrick and Laeghaire. Lochru went fiercely, enviously, with contention and questions, against Patrick; and then he began to denounce the Trinity and the Catholic faith. Patrick looked severely at him, and cried out to God with a loud voice, and he said: '*Domine qui omnia potes et in tua potestate consistit quidquid est, quique nos misisti huc ad nomen tuum gentibus praedicandum hic impius qui blasphemat nomen tuum, elevatur nunc foras, et cito moriatur. Et his dictis elevatus est magus in aëra et iterum desuper cito dejectus sparso ad lapidem cerebro comminutus et mortus fuerat coram eis.*' The pagans became afraid at this. But the king was much infuriated against Patrick, and he determined to kill him. He told his people to slay the cleric. When Patrick observed this thing – the rising up against him of the pagans – he cried out with a loud voice, and said: '*Et exurget Deus et dissipentur inimici ejus, et fugiant qui oderunt eum a facie ejus, sicut deficit fumus deficit sic deficiant sicut fluit caera a facie ignis; sic pereint peccatorus facie Domini.*' Immediately darkness went over the sun, and great shaking and trembling of the earth occurred. They thought it was heaven that fell upon the earth; and the horses started off, frightened, and the wind blew the chariots across the plains, and all rose against each other in the assembly; and they were all attacking each other, so that fifty men of them fell in this commotion through Patrick's malediction. The Gentiles fled in all directions, so that only three remained – viz., Laeghaire, and his queen, and a man of his people; *et timuerunt valde, veniensque regina ad Patricium* (*i.e.*, Angass, daughter of Tassagh, son of Liathan), dixit: '*Ei homo juste et potens ne perdas regem.* The king will go to thee, and will submit to thee, and will kneel, and will believe in God.' Laeghaire went then, and knelt before Patrick, and gave him a '*false peace*'. Not long after this, the king beckoned Patrick aside, and what he meditated was to kill him; but this happened not, because God had manifested this intention to Patrick. Laeghaire said to Patrick, 'Come after me, O cleric! to Tara, that I may believe in thee before the men of Erinn'; and he then placed men in ambush before Patrick in every pass from Ferta-fer-féc to Tara, that they might kill him. But God did not permit it. Patrick went, accompanied by eight young clerics (*maccleirech*), and Benen as a *gilla*, along with them; and Patrick blessed them before going, and a *dicheltair* (garment of invisibility) went over them, so that not one of them was seen. The Gentiles who were in the ambuscades, however, saw eight wild deer going past them along the mountain, and a young fawn after them, and a pouch on his shoulder – viz., Patrick, and his eight [clerics], and Benen after them, and his (Patrick's) *polaire* (satchel, or epistolary) on his back.

Laeghaire went afterwards, about twilight, to Tara, in sorrow and shame, with the few persons who escaped in his company. On the day succeeding Easter Sunday the men of Erinn went to Tara to drink the feast; for the *Fes* of Tara was a principal day with them. When they were banqueting, and thinking of the conflict they waged the day before, they saw Patrick, who arrived in the middle of Tara, *januis clausis ut Christus in cennaculum*; because

Patrick meditated: 'I will go,' said he, 'so that my readiness may be manifested before the men of Erinn. I shall not make a candle under a bushel of myself. I will see,' said he, 'who will believe me, and who will not believe me.' No one rose up before him inside but *Dubhtach* Mac Ua Lugair alone, the king's royal poet, and a tender youth of his people (viz., his name was Fiacc; it is he who is [commemorated] in Slebhte to-day). This Dubhtach, truly, was the first man who believed that day in Tara. Patrick blessed him and his seed.

Anon.
The Tripartite Life of Saint Patrick
Translated by Whitley Stokes, 1887

St Patrick's Rock, Cashel

The buildings which crown St Patrick's Rock present a mass and outline of great interest and beauty hardly equaled – in these islands – by that of the castle rock at Edinburgh or surpassed, further afield, by those of Mont St Michel or Le Puy in France.

H.G. Leask

Though lacking the massive and military character of the Scottish site and the spires 'whose silent finger points to Heaven' in Normandy and Auvergne, the Irish Group has a character of its own, unique and native, and is one of the most remarkable in Europe.

Earliest and most lofty of the Cashel edifices is the tenth century Round Tower, a very perfectly preserved example, while next in date stands the famous Chapel of King Cormac, consecrated in 1134. Joining these buildings, and stretching out to east and west beyond them, lies the roofless cathedral, built between 1235 and 1270, crowned by a massive tower – perhaps of the fourteenth century – and terminating, at its western end, in the strong archiepiscopal castle built a century later. The only isolated structure, that through which the visitor enters, is the Hall of the Vicars-Choral, which is also an erection of the fifteenth century.

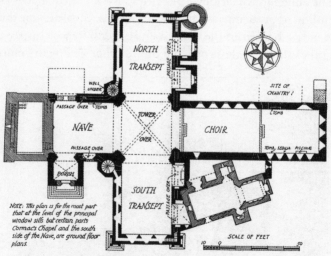

NOTE: This plan is for the most part that at the level of the principal window sills but certain parts Cormac's Chapel and the south side of the Nave, are ground floor plans.

SCALE OF FEET

ST. PATRICK'S ROCK, CASHEL: PLAN OF THE CATHEDRAL.

H.G. Leask

The Rock of Cashel, rising so commandingly over the fertile 'Golden Vale', must have offered a splendid site for a fortress from the earliest times; it is, indeed, as a fortress, a dún, or caiseal, that we first hear of it. Corc, first of the name, that almost legendary king of Munster – descended from Eophan, the eldest son of Oilioll Olum – seems to have flourished in the fourth century. He is credited with the foundation of his capital at Cashel about 370 A.D. The rocky site he chose for this was known as Sidh Dhruim: the Fairy Ridge, before he built his caiseal of unmortared stone upon it. From that time onwards to the beginning of the twelfth century 'Cashel of the Kings' remained a chief residence of the Munster monarchs ...

In 1101 Cashel was granted to the Church. The Annals of the Four Masters tell us that 'a meeting of Leath Mogha (i.e., Munster) was held at Cashel by Muirceartach Ua Briain, with the chiefs of the laity, and Ua Dunain, noble bishop and senior, with the chiefs of the Clergy'. On this occasion Ua Briain made a grant, 'such as no king ever before made, namely, he granted Caiseal of the Kings to the Religious'. It was dedicated to God, St. Patrick and St. Ailbe.

H.G. Leask
St Patrick's Rock, Cashel, 1933

St. Patrick and Louth: Patrick's First Visit

If, as the *Tripartite* would have us believe, Patrick entered Louth during his first preaching in eastern Bregia, that visit must be ascribed to the year 433. It is difficult to come to any safe judgment about this visit. While the *Tripartite* is very explicit on the point, none of the other lives mention it. The *Tripartite* tells us that after leaving Tara Patrick founded Trim, in which he placed St. Loman, and many other churches. The narrative then says: 'He also built the church called Druiminiscleann, which afterwards became celebrated and in which now lie two of his disciples – Dalruanus and Lugadius son of Aengus King of Cashel.' That the reference in this passage is to Dromiskin in County Louth there cannot be any doubt. Not only is Druiminiscleann the Irish name for Dromiskin, but from the *Martyrology of Donegal* and the *Martyrology of Marianus O'Gorman*, as well as from other reliable sources, we know that St. Lugadius son of Aengus King of Cashel died at Dromiskin, and that his feast was kept there on the 2nd November. There are, however, difficulties in the way of accepting the story told by the *Tripartite* author. In the list of churches, among which Druiminiscleann is mentioned, the remaining ones are all in County Meath, and the nearest of them is almost twenty miles from Dromiskin. All the other churches are within a short distance from Tara, which was St. Patrick's headquarters for the time. If St. Patrick took upon himself this extra journey of twenty miles it seems likely that he would have founded more churches than one. For these reasons many writers think that St. Patrick did not enter Louth at this time, and that the *Tripartite* author mistook Dromiskin for some place in County Meath with a similar name – possibly Dunshaughlin. Professor Bury, the latest writer on St. Patrick, is of this opinion. On the other hand, Whitley Stokes, whose judgment is rarely at fault, is content to accept Dromiskin in County Louth. Dr. Healy, although he almost invariably follows the *Tripartite* narrative, does not mention the matter. Lanigan suggests Drumshallon in County Louth instead of Dromiskin. This suggestion would get us over the difficulty concerning the distance, but Drumshallon never was called Druiminiscleann, nor would it answer the description given in the *Tripartite*. Colgan, whom difficulties of time and place never disturbed, accepts the *Tripartite* narrative without any comment. After a careful consideration of both sides, I feel inclined to believe that

St. Patrick did come to Dromiskin. The *Tripartite* narrative, at the first point, is concerned with events which happened during the first year of Patrick's preaching, when helpers were few and when there was no thought of writing a life of the Saint. In after years, when the time did come for writing an account of Patrick's works, few, if any, eye-witnesses of the early labours were living. This may be given as a reason for the confused account found, in the *Tripartite*, of this part of St. Patrick's labour, so unlike the more orderly accounts of the missions in Connaught and Ulster. Many of the Meath churches mentioned in the list have remained unidentified. Dromiskin was probably remembered, because, when the *Tripartite* account was written, it had grown into a flourishing monastery, and the monks had carried on the tradition of Patrick's visit; but the other places in County Louth through which he had passed were forgotten. We must remember, too, that the territory of Magh Breagh or Bregia extended as far as Dromiskin, and it is to be expected that when Patrick took up the work of preaching in the territory, he visited each part of it. Furthermore, the *Vita Tripartite* is the most complete and most valuable of the Lives, and, although in its present form it cannot have been written earlier than the twelfth century, still it is certain that an old life written in the sixth century by St. Evin, of Monastereven, was used extensively in its compilation.

Some of the details of this visit to County Louth can be filled in from other sources. The *Tripartite* account explains, and is at the same time confirmed by the description given in the life of St. Dachonna of the founding of the monastery of Doire Disirt Dachonna, now known as Dysart in the Barony of Ferrard. Of St. Patrick's connection with this monastery no mention is made in any of the Lives, but in the Life of St. Dachonna it is stated that, early in his missionary career, St. Patrick founded Dysart. Dachonna, whom he afterwards placed over the monastery, was a native of County Louth, and was formerly honoured on the

12th April. Unless we admit the truth of St. Patrick's visit to Dromiskin we cannot explain the founding of Dysart by him. This was Patrick's only visit to East Louth; never afterwards did he come east of the great road of Midluachair, which ran from Slane, west of Collon, through Ardee and on to Dundalk.

The *Tripartite* narrative receives further confirmation from the strong tradition, formerly existing, that Patrick, early in his career, visited Drogheda and founded a monastery there. In the Lives there is no mention of Patrick having visited Drogheda, except perhaps on his way to Slane, and he certainly did not found a monastery there at that time. The tradition, however, that the mediaeval Augustinian Abbey on the bank of the Boyne near the West Gate was built on the ground upon which formerly a Patrician Monastery had stood, is too strong to be lightly set aside. If we admit the visit to Dromiskin, we can easily explain the founding of the Drogheda monastery.

Lorcán Ua Muireadhaigh
Journal of the County Louth Archaeological Society, 1910

Saint Patrick in Munster

The *Tripartite* records that there were idols at Cashel, and that they were found prostrated on the morning after the arrival of the saint. He was welcomed by Aengus, son of Nadfraech, and many of the men of Munster, upon whom he invoked a special blessing. During the ceremony, St. Patrick inadvertently pierced the foot of Aengus with the point of his crozier. The brave young prince bore the pain in silence, and, when the saint inquired afterwards why he had not complained, he replied that he thought 'it was the rule of Faith', or a part of the usual ceremony. Such a noble instance of devotion could not pass unrewarded, and special benedictions were bestowed upon him and his race …

The saint now continued his journey towards the south, until he arrived in the present county Limerick. After passing through Aradha-Cliach, he went on to Jochtar-Cuillen, where he restored a child to life, who had been killed by pigs. He desired Malach Britt, a Céle-De of his people, to resuscitate him; but this man had not the faith or the obedience necessary for so great a work, and another gained his crown. Patrick now commanded Bishops Ibar and Ailbhe to perform the miracle, and he prayed with them. As might be expected, after such a notable event, all the people of Ui-Cuanach believed.

At Grean a number of women came to the saint, and bewailed his departure, and he gave them a special blessing. Many of the most remarkable incidents in the life of the saint are connected with his visit to Limerick and its neighborhood. A very curious incident is related about the foundation of the church of Mungret, which lies about three miles south-west of the city. Lonan, son of Mac Erc, made a banquet for him on top of Cae, a mountain in Hy-Figente.

A deacon, named Mantan, who is described as one of Patrick's people, was assisting in the preparation of the feast, and a troop of jugglers came to the saint to ask for food, and would take no excuse. He sent them to Lonan and Mantan, but they refused to give them food, which was an act of contempt to the order of the saint, and was punished as such …

Mantan, the deacon, was informed that his church would never be held in honor. Nessan was instructed by the saint, and baptized, and eventually established in the church, and this, says the writer, came to pass, for her grave is in the west of Mungarret, and the bell of the great church is not heard in that place.

Nessan and his church were to be 'honored among the nations'; and it is not a little remarkable that the Limerick people have ever manifested not only an unwavering fidelity to the true faith, but have also been amongst the most gallant defenders of the sacred deposit then bestowed upon them. They still cherish the memory of St. Patrick with tender devotion, and point proudly to the various sites in their county where memorials of the saint are found in the names, still preserved, of the places which he visited …

At Patrick's Well, near Limerick, which still retains its name and holy traditions, the prince of the Desi came late to the assembly for which Patrick was waiting. He excused himself on account of the rain, but the excuse did not satisfy the saint, who predicted that all his meetings for the future should be attended by showers. Singland is situated in the parish of St. Patrick, about an English mile from the city of Limerick; and, in the Cromwellian and Williamite wars, was frequently the headquarters of the invading forces. It was from the heights of Singland that the canons of Ireton, in 1651, and of William and Ginkle, forty years after, played upon the 'Black Battery', and citadel of Limerick.

St. Patrick's next journey was into Muscraidhe Tire, where he met three brothers, men of note, sons of Forat MacCoula, one of whom, Munechus, believed at once, and was baptized. To him special temporal blessings were promised.

The time at last came when the mission of our apostle was accomplished in Munster, and he must leave that faithful people, to do his master's work elsewhere amongst the devoted men of Erinn. He bid them farewell, and left a blessing with them; but they could not bear to part thus from the saint, whom they had learned to revere so deeply. Patrick went to Brosna, but crowds still followed him from all quarters. The very hills seemed in motion, so great was the multitude who hastened along, heedless of all difficulties, to get one more glimpse of their venerable father and their friend. When they saw him they made the mountains re-echo with their shouts of joy, and then another miracle was granted to their faith and fervor, for they beheld the resuscitation of a Munsterman who had been dead for seven-and-twenty years. A holy bishop, named Frion, who is graphically described as a son of devotion, gave a banquet to the assembled multitudes, which St. Patrick blessed, and by another miracle satisfied all who were present; and then, once more, and for the last time on earth, he blessed the men of Munster, saying:

> A blessing on the men of Munster.
> A blessing on the land which gives them food.
> A blessing on whatever is produced for its farmers.
> A blessing on each chief.
> A blessing on the men of Munster.
> A blessing on their woods,
> A blessing on their sloping plains,
> A blessing on their glens,
> A blessing on their hills.
> A blessing of sand beneath their ships.
> A blessing of numerous homesteads.
> A blessing on their slopes and levels.
> A blessing on their slieves and peaks.
> A blessing.

M.F. Cusack
Life of Saint Patrick: Apostle of Ireland, 1871

A Pilgrimage to Croagh Patrick
July 31, 1910

It is now many years ago since a very laudable desire began to grow and strengthen within the present writer of making, when opportunity offered, a pilgrimage to the soaring summit of Croagh Patrick, that hallowed spot which, beyond all doubt, has been sanctified for all time by the blessed feet of our own great National Patron and Apostle, Patrick, who preached 'the gospel of peace' and brought 'glad tidings of good things' to our pagan forefathers.

However, not until the present year of grace, AD 1910, did circumstances permit the accomplishment of the aforesaid laudable and long-cherished desire …

The present writer will venture to give a very imperfect and altogether unofficial account of a truly remarkable and edifying pilgrimage.

AT THE FOOT OF CROAGH PATRICK.

Postcard *c.*1910 showing pilgrims at the foot of
Croagh Patrick, County Mayo.

'The Annual Pilgrimage to Croagh Patrick takes place always on the last Sunday in July.' Such is the authentic announcement. And so it came to pass that, on the last Sunday of July, AD 1910, on the last day of the month, and on the Feast of St. Ignatius, we (a congenial fellow-pilgrim priest and myself) had not only the genuine Christian happiness of struggling up that steep and rugged mountain side, through cloud and mist, in company with thousands of earnest and devout pilgrims from many lands, but also the special privilege of offering up the Holy Sacrifice of the Mass in the beautiful little oratory of Templepatrick which so befittingly crowns the towering summit of this holy mountain, a mountain the very holiest as well as the very fairest in the land. With good reason it has been compared to Mount Sinai, and, indeed, with equally good reason it might be compared even to the sacred Mount of Calvary itself. But we must descend from those holy heights, and, without further preamble, begin at the beginning of our pilgrimage.

Well, we arrived at Westport by train in the forenoon of Saturday, July 30th, and were welcomed at the station by a kindly young priest whom Canon M'Donald, in his own absence, had thoughtfully sent to meet us.

Having arranged about our rooms at a good, comfortable hotel, and after taking a turn through the picturesque and interesting town of Westport (one of the capitals of Co. Mayo), with its quaint old bridges and beautiful river and embankments overshadowed by noble trees, and after a short stroll in Lord Sligo's fine demesne, which that nobleman has generously thrown open to the public – in a word, after doing all this, we called upon our friend, Canon M'Donald ... 'We should,' he said, 'consider his house as our own during our stay – should dine with him, take tea with him (for we are all teetotalers), should come in and go out as we pleased.' Accordingly, at five o'clock, we had to come, dine with him and meet His Grace Archbishop Healy, who had just arrived, after driving almost all the day long in order to take part in and encourage by his presence the celebration of the pilgrimage tomorrow. Needless to say that the zealous and learned Archbishop and his worthy Administrator, Canon M'Donald (now promoted P.P. of

Newport), have laboured long and earnestly to revive and place on solid, religious and approved foundations this most ancient and salutary pilgrimage of Croagh Patrick.

During and after dinner there was some speculation on the condition of the mountain under foot, at present, for climbing and the prospects of fine weather for the morrow.

The Canon, who presided at table, declared that he was almost worn out praying for a fine day! The Archbishop then mentioned that, even in the oldest records of the pilgrimage, the elements were sometimes most unpropitious, and pilgrims accordingly often suffered great hardships, and on the occasion of a pilgrimage to Croagh Patrick on the Saint's own Feast Day AD 1113 we are told that thirty of 'the fasting folk' perished in a thunderstorm on the mountain on the night of the 17th of March.

This being so, we may well believe that the great Apostle and lover of the Irish race had both the will and the power with God of changing this apparent calamity into an everlasting blessing for the souls of those poor 'fasting folk' who perished on such a good day and in such a good cause. The Archbishop also mentioned that Cardinal Logue had intended to take part in the pilgrimage this year, and climb even to the very summit of the Reek; but, added His Grace, we succeeded (and it was no easy matter) in dissuading His Eminence from carrying out his good intentions. The Cardinal met their objection on the score of age by stating that his great predecessor, St. Patrick, at the time he ascended the Reek, was, according to the best authorities, almost exactly the same age as he (the Cardinal) himself was at the present time. (Cardinal Logue was born October 1st, AD 1840.) Perhaps it was better that the Cardinal did not venture on the pilgrimage this year, for the morning broke dull and grey, and heavy rain clouds and mist and fog enveloped and concealed the upper heights of the holy mountain almost all day long from view, and many even of the hardy peasants of the locality, who have been accustomed from youth to make this pilgrimage annually, declared that they never found the ascent to the summit more difficult than it was this present year.

On Saturday evening the priests who wished to say Mass on the summit entered their names in a register kept at the presbytery, Westport, and both the hour and the altar at which each priest was to say Mass in the Oratory were appointed. The Archbishop also gave to all approved confessors faculties to hear the confessions of pilgrims on the holy mountain the following morning, and very many of the pilgrims, for their spiritual strength and comfort, availed themselves to the opportunity thus afforded them.

The Oratory, of course, is dedicated to St. Patrick, and there are three altars in the sanctuary thereof; the high altar is that of St. Patrick, and is surmounted by a handsome statue of our National Apostle ...

The altar on the Epistle side of the high altar is dedicated to the Most Sacred Heart of Jesus, and the third altar on the Gospel side is dedicated to the Blessed Virgin Mary ...

An important consideration, in connexion with the pilgrimage of Croagh Patrick, is the matter of dress, for a suitable style of dress makes the greatest possible difference as to comfort and ease in mountain climbing; and, in the case of Croagh Patrick, rather rough mountain climbing at the best.

Low, thin-soled shoes are not the thing where one frequently sinks above the ankles in wet, boggy turf loam, and ladies' fashionable high-heeled boots are, to say the very least of them, quite at a discount where loose, sharp rocks and stones, and heaps of them, covering long and steep stretches of the 'Pilgrim's Path', have to be got over somehow. For gentlemen we would recommend good, thick-soled boots (not shoes), with a few spikes or nails to prevent slipping, leggings of some sort, a light, rainproof cape, and a good, long, reliable walking-stick or pilgrim's staff. Canon M'Donald recommended and kindly gave the handle of a sweeping brush, with a prepared point, to one of our pilgrim priests, who found it to be of the greatest service both in going up and coming down the Reek. With regard to a suitable dress or outfit for ladies, we shall attempt to give only very little and very negative advice, namely, in the first place, not to wear light-soled, high-heeled shoes or boots; and, in the second place, not to wear over-long skirts, which cling about the feet, and, when the mountain is wet under foot or when there is rain and mist (which seems to be oftener the case than not), soon become very bedraggled and uncomfortable …

It was half-past seven o'clock on Sunday morning that four of us started on an outside car from Westport, through Lord Sligo's demesne, to Murrisk, with its venerable old Augustinian Abbey, the starting place proper of the pilgrimage …

Immediately on our arrival at Murrisk we entered on the ancient 'Pilgrim's Path' and began our ascent; and immediately also, on beginning our ascent, a feeling took possession of us that we had now indeed entered upon holy ground. For were we not treading the very path which Patrick himself trod? and were we not following him in spirit and in truth, to the summit of the holy mountain where he 'spent' himself for us, in prayer and fasting, during the forty long days of Lent? In this connexion, how touching are the simple words of St. Patrick himself, taken from the golden book of his 'Confession':

> I spent myself for you that you might receive me, and both amongst yourselves and wherever I journeyed for your sake, through many perils, even in remote parts where no man dwelt, and where no one had ever come to baptize or ordain clergy, or confirm the people, I have through God's goodness done everything carefully and most willingly for your salvation … Wherefore may it never happen to me from God that I should ever lose His people [the Irish] whom He hath purchased at the ends of the earth.

Such words as these brace one to overcome difficulties of every kind. So let us return with renewed energy to our ascent of the Holy Reek ...

It takes about two hours to climb from Murrisk to the summit, when the conditions are favourable, but it took us longer by reason of the unfavourable condition of the mountain under foot, caused by recent heavy rains, and also by reason of the thick mist and fog which, until late in the afternoon, lay like a heavy mantle over the shoulders of the mountain.

We soon began to overtake and pass some of the more aged and the more weakly of the pilgrims, who had started long before us. One fine old fellow, going on sticks, told us that he was eighty years of age, had come from Ballyhaunis by train, had walked out from Westport, and hoped to get to the top in time to hear Father M'Grath's sermon. We helped him over some difficult passages, and in one place, after stumbling on the rocks and recovering himself somewhat, he said, 'Sure it's nothing to what our Blessed Saviour suffered going up Mount Calvary.' There was nothing gloomy, morose or selfish in the conduct of the pilgrims, but, on the contrary, a splendid spirit of true Christian gentleness and fortitude – the strong and courageous willing and anxious to help the weak and timid. So remarkable and edifying, indeed, was this spirit, that some of our pilgrim priests who had been lately through the Holy Land, and at Oberammergau, as well as at some of the most famous shrines of pilgrimage we read of, declared that they were more deeply moved and impressed by the simple faith and piety of the pilgrims on Croagh Patrick than by anything they had witnessed in foreign lands.

After about an hour's climbing we began to meet many of those who had already been to the summit and were now returning. Some of the older people had gone up the evening before, and had spent the night on the mountain side, or praying around the Oratory on the summit, and indeed they must have suffered greatly throughout that wet and dreary night, and no wonder they should look weary and faint and worn after having been 'buffeted at will by rain and storm' all night long during their vigil on such a wild and shelterless mountain.

We asked one poor feeble old man, who was descending with much difficulty, whether he had gone to the top or not. 'No,' he replied, with sorrow in his voice, 'the heart failed me, and I had to turn back'.

The next we accosted was a vigorous young fellow who was coming down 'strong'. 'Are we near the top?' one of us asked him. 'Begorrah, Father,' said he, 'you have two good miles *of it* before you yet.' This, we may remark, was an exceptional reply, by no means encouraging, but the replies in general were 'kindly Irish' of the Irish, and well calculated to cheer and revive the drooping spirits, such as 'Bravo! you're getting on grand, you have only a few hundred yards more to climb,' or, 'Take your time, *alanna*, and you'll soon be at the top,' etc. Then we met a poor fellow with a handkerchief tied around his head and blood oozing from underneath it. What happened him? Well, he told us that he was on the mountain since one o'clock in the morning, and that when coming down from the summit he slipped and fell among the rocks.

At one of the most trying parts of the ascent we came upon some Dublin gentlemen, evidently tired out and resting on the hard rocks. 'Are you going up or coming down?' one of us asked them. 'Bedad! We're going up to Mass, Father,' they replied, adding good-humouredly, 'but this place is very different from Clarendon Street.'

At length, after a long and hard struggle, our clothes drenched with rain, our feet wet, our boots and lower garments covered with clammy turf-mould, we reached the towering summit of the stony, verdureless pyramid of Croagh Patrick (2,510 feet). Weary, indeed, and somewhat uncomfortable we felt, to be sure, but, at the same time, our hearts were beating high with feelings of gratitude and triumph, arising, no doubt, from the fact that we had 'spent' ourselves a little for our soul's sake, and were, to some extent, co-operating with St. Patrick, who was able to confess, at the close of his long and laborious life, that he had 'through God's goodness done everything carefully and most willingly for [our] salvation'.

The priests who said their Masses early heard a good many of the pilgrims' confessions afterwards, and at the time we entered the little Oratory of Templepatrick, rows of pious pilgrims were receiving Holy Communion, and there were pilgrims for Communion at the Masses until after mid-day.

A Spanish priest said Mass at eleven o'clock on the high altar dedicated to St. Patrick; another priest, who was to have said Mass at that same altar and at the same hour, yielded his claim, in consideration of the fact that the brave young Spanish priest had not only climbed the Reek fasting, but had, moreover, walked out all the way from Westport that morning. We noticed that whilst the *Spaniard* was saying Mass at St. Patrick's altar, there was an *American* saying Mass at the Sacred Heart altar, and an *Irishman* saying Mass at the Blessed Virgin's altar, all at the same time, thus very worthily representing the good Catholic peoples of three nationalities. One of our priests, who said Mass at the Virgin's altar, was much edified and not a little distracted by observing one or two young country girls coming gently forward and placing bunches of nice fresh flowers on the altar at which he was celebrating. God bless them for their goodness and foresight! – for those flowers never grew on the mountain, and must have been brought up with that pious intention from the valley below.

There was a Protestant lady also who made this pilgrimage and brought her little daughter (a Catholic) up along with her to the summit of the Reek. May God enlighten and move that good mother to embrace, in all its fullness, the same true Catholic faith which St. Patrick preached!

After our Masses we were indeed very grateful for some sandwiches and a warm cup of tea nicely prepared for us (thanks to Canon M'Donald) by two or three young ladies from the Technical School, Westport. If we could remember the names of these good Samaritans we should be delighted to give them honourable mention here; all we can remember with certainty about them is, that one of them was from the County Wexford and another from the County Cork. But their names will all appear, on one great day, please God, in the Book of Life.

E. O'L
The Irish Monthly, 1910

The Wood of Foclut

Perhaps the knottiest problem in the story of St. Patrick as it has come down to us is that concerning the Wood of Foclut.

The primal source of the reference to this wood occurs in the Saint's own Confession. Let us quote the passage –

> And again after a few years I was in Britain with my kindred … and there verily I saw in the night visions a man, whose name was Victoricus, coming as it were from Ireland with countless letters. And he gave me one of them, and I read the beginning of the letter, which was entitled 'The Voice of the Irish', and while I was reading aloud the beginning of the letter, I thought that at that very moment I heard the voice of them who lived beside the Wood of Foclut which is nigh unto the western sea. And thus they cried, as with one mouth, 'We beseech thee, holy youth, to come and walk among us once more.' And I was exceedingly broken in heart, and could read no further. And so I awoke.

The difficulty which is raised by this item of the Saint's autobiography is due to the fact that ever since Tirechan's time this Wood of Foclut is understood to have been a wood near Killala in the Co. Mayo; and the passage above quoted clearly shows that St. Patrick, during his period of slavery in Ireland, had known the people who lived beside this wood, even to recognising their voices, while they in turn beg him to walk once more amongst them, implying that he had done so before. And how this could be so of a slave who had spent all his six years of slavery in Co. Antrim is a perplexity which has puzzled all our scholars, and called forth a great variety of solutions – some of them amazingly improbable.

Lanigan suggests that he went there (to Killala) with his master to buy or sell pigs!

Dr. Healy quite properly ridicules this idea, and gives his own explanation, that when Patrick fled from his master he went westward and embarked at Killala.

Dr. Bury sees the double absurdity of this, first that the message in the letter 'implies a previous sojourning far more protracted than the day or two spent at the port in waiting for the vessel to sail'; and second, 'that a flight from the west to an eastern port is what we should expect rather than a flight from the east coast to a western harbour'. Dr. White also says 'It is extremely unlikely that any of the ports of commerce between Ireland and Britain, or Ireland and the Continent, were on the west coast.' It is curious how each author can see the weakness in the other's argument but not in his own ...

My main object in this paper is to call farther attention to an article which appeared in the 'The Catholic Bulletin' of March, 1917, dealing with this question ...

The gist of the article was that there was a place-name in Co. Antrim, near the village of Cushendall, and only half a mile from the sea, called Faughil; that this meant Fó-chaill, an underwood or shrubbery whence the large trees had been removed. Then the writer argued that Patrick was near enough at Slemish to make the acquaintance of youths at Faughil and to contract friendships with them, and even make converts among them, so that when at home again in Britain his mind in his waking hours was recalling these young friends of his days of servitude, and dreaming about them at night, and that this was the real Foclut Wood of Patrick's dream and not one in distant Connacht which he had never seen. He also pointed out that 'the western sea' to a man of Roman ideas did not connote the sea west of Ireland, but the sea west of Britain or even west of Europe, so that a place near the sea in Co. Antrim would come within such a description …

With Foclut within a reasonable distance of Slemish, 'not too near for familiarity or too far for friendship', the story of Patrick's acquaintance with the youth there, his interest in them, and his subsequent dreaming of them is quite natural and understandable, and needs no theories whatever.

Henry Morris
Down and Connor Historical Society's Journal, 1937

The Prophecy of the Saint Concerning Dublinia

And the saint, departing from Midia, directed his course toward Lagenia, for the purpose of preaching there; and on his journey he crossed a river named Finglas to a certain hill distant about one mile from the village Athcliath, the which is now called Dublinia; and looking on this place and on the country around it, and blessing it, thus spake he, prophesying: 'This village, now so small in time shall be renowned, and it shall be increased in riches and in dignity until it be advanced the royal seat of the kingdom.' How truly he spake the proof of this time manifestly showeth. And he entered the village, and the dwellers therein, having heard of the miracles which he had wrought in the Lord, came forth joyfully to meet him; and the son of the lord of that place, his only son, was even at the point of death, so that many said he had already expired. Then, at the entreaty of the father and of the rest who flocked around him, the saint went unto the sick man's bed, and bended his knees on the earth, and prayed, and blessed him then dying, and snatched him from the jaws of death, and in the sight of them all restored him.

Jocelin
Life and Acts of Saint Patrick
Translated by Edmund L. Swift
The Most Ancient Lives of Saint Patrick, 1874

Lough Derg

From Cavan and from Leitrim and from Mayo,
From all the thin-faced parishes where hills
Are perished noses running peaty water,
They come to Lough Derg to fast and pray and beg
With all the bitterness of nonentities, and the envy
Of the inarticulate when dealing with the artist.
Their hands push closed the doors that God holds open;
Love-sunlit is an enchanter in June's hours
And flowers and light. These to shopkeepers and small lawyers
Are heresies up beauty's sleeve.
The naive and simple go on pilgrimage too,
Lovers trying to take God's truth for granted …
Listen to the chanted
Evening devotions in the limestone church,
For this is Lough Derg, St Patrick's Purgatory.

Patrick Kavanagh
Lough Derg, 1978

The Form of Penance to be Performed at Patrick's Purgatory in Lough Derg

When you come in sight of the Island wherein stands St. Patrick's Purgatory you are to uncover both head and feet and so continue until you come into the Island.

At ye entrance into ye Island ye must kneel at ye great Alter of St. Patrick and there say upon yr knees one Pater, Ave and Credo.

And you are barefooted and bareheaded to surround the Alter three times and say three Paters, three Aves and Credo.

Then you are to surround the chappell seven times with a Rosary of seven Decates, and every time as you go about you are to lean your back to a broad stone in the wall, where ye whole time of ye penance you must be bareheaded and barefooted.

And from ye chappell you must goe to ye seven penitentiall saints' beds and kneel within the first bed and say three Paters, three Aves and Credo; and then you are to surround the seven beds within and without, saying three Paters, three Aves and Credo.

And from the saints' beds you are to go to the Logh where there is a great stone within the Logh and where St. Patrick leaned his knee, and you are to surround that stone three times, saying three Aves, three Paters and Credo.

And from the stone within the Logh to the stone without the Logh [on which] St. Patrick stood and left the mark of his feet and there you must stand, saying three Paters, three Aves and Credo.

And from thence to the great alter where you began kneeling and saying Pater, Ave and Credo, and from there to the chappell saying the Rosary of the 15 Decates; and this whole penance is to be performed three times every day for eight days together, only the refreshment of bread and water once every day.

And the 8th day you are to goe to the Prior and make Confession and receive the Sacrament and get absolution.

The statue of St Patrick at Lough Derg

And then you are to enter St. Patrick's Purgatory, which is an artificial cave above ground, narrow at the entrance, but somewhat wider at the further end, where you can but only kneel, and there you are to remain kneeling for the space of twenty-four hours without any refreshment of meat or drink and without sleep.

After your coming out of Purgatory, you must goe to the alter in the chappell and hear Mass and give your devotion to the Prior, and then goe and wash yourself three times in the Logh and get the Prior's benediction and goe away as you came bareheaded and barefooted until you be out of the Island.

Anon.
Journal of the County Louth Archaeological Society, 1910

A Place Where Neighbour
Reaches Out To Neighbour

Among the many persecutions against Catholics, the penal laws included a ban on pilgrimages to places such as Lough Derg on Co. Donegal's border with Fermanagh.

The reality was somewhat different, or at least it was when Dr Hugh McMahon, the Catholic Bishop of Clogher, wrote of the 'extraordinary' way in which Protestants and Catholics in the area did not interfere in one another's worship.

'Every year thousands of men and women of all ages come from even the most distant parts of the country to this island to make a novena,' he wrote in 1714.

'During the three months of the pilgrimage season Masses are being celebrated continuously from dawn till midday.

'An extraordinary feature of the pilgrimage is that none of the Protestants in the locality ever interfere with the pilgrims, although people are forbidden by law of parliament to make it.'

This had profound implications, Bishop McMahon said.

'The result is that, while in the rest of the country the practice of religion has practically ceased as a result of persecution, here, as in another world, religion is practiced feely and openly,' he wrote.

That spirit of cooperation continues today. In recent years in particular, Lough Derg – although very much under the auspices of a Catholic prior – has made great efforts to embrace Protestant pilgrims, including hosting events with speakers from the Reformed Churches.

In part this is an acknowledgement that Lough Derg has been part of Irish Christian tradition for more than 1,000 years, and thus pre-dates the Reformation. But it also reflects the belief that 'neighbour can reach out to neighbour'.

William Scholes
Irish News, 13 February 2014

A Description of St. Patrick's Purgatory

The whole Island is a rocky Piece of Ground, in some Places bare, and in the rest having but a very thin Covering of Earth. It is in Length 126 Yards, in the broadest Place 45, and narrowest 22 over. The most convenient Landing Place is on the South-East Side, where the first Thing remarkable that occurs is St. Patrick's altar, with an old crois within a Circle on it, inscribed *Jacobus Grah fieri fecit*, 1632. *Jocelin*, in the Life of St. Patrick, saith, that the Pope presented him with a stone altar, which had not only the Faculty of Swimming it self, but also of transporting others, of which St. Patrick made the following Experiment. As he was about to sail from Britain to Ireland, a leper begg'd earnestly to be admitted into the Ship, which the Seamen refusing, he threw this Altar to him; upon which he had a safe Passage, and landed at this same time with those in the Ship. Whether it be pretended that this is the same Altar, I cannot tell; but it is probable, that this Story might have brought any Thing, that is called St. Patrick's altar into great Esteem in Ireland. Next to this altar is a ruinous Church, 40 Foot long and 11 broad. The Chappel is an isle on the South side of the church, 16 foot Square. It hath been partly repaired of late, and covered with heath. It is open on the Side next to the old church; and hath an Altar on the South side, 4 foot high, covered with a flat Stone, on the Corner the figure of *Caoranach* is placed, which is drawn like a Wolf (the most Pernicious animal in *Ireland*), with Serpent's tail between its Legs, and thrown over its Back. The Cave, commonly called *St. Patrick's Purgatory* ... and celebrated by some Writers of the Church of Rome (and especially *Petrus Lombardus*) as the most holy and most memorable Place in Ireland, is about 10 Foot distant from the Church; it is 22 Foot long, 2 Foot and 1 Inch wide, and 3 Foot high; it hath a bending within 6 Foot of the far End, where there is a very small Window or Spike hole to let in some Light and Air to the *Pilgrims* that are shut up in it. There is little or none of it under Ground, and it seems never to have been sunk deeper than the Rock. It is built of Stone and Clay hudled together, covered with broad Stones, and all overlaid with Earth; so very different is this renowned Pit, as it is falsely stiled in the Legends, from the Accounts there given of it. The six Circles are commonly called the seven Saints penitential Beds, viz. St. Brenans, St. Catherines, St. Brigids, St. Columbs St. Moluis, and St. Patricks, and St. Aveogs; they are some 9, some 10, and some 11 Foot diameter, but St. Patricks is 16, for *Moluis* and he lay together: their walls are about 2 foot high, every one of them having a small Gap for an Entrance into it. The *Irish* believe, that these Saints lay several Nights upon these Beds by way of Penance for their own Sins, and the Sins of the People; which if true, the Hardness of their lodging made the Penance very severe; for they are so rugged and thick set with small pointed Stones, that the greatest Saint in the Church of Rome could not bear it now, and much less take any rest upon them. The Altar of Confession is in the remotest Part of the Island. The Stones lying near one another, part above and part under Water, are the Monsters metamorphosed Guts. The Stone about 2 Foot and a half under water, is called *leacna mbonn*, that is a flat Stone for the Soles of the Feet. It is smooth, having a hole in the middle, in which there is another Stone like the Stump of a Broken Cross. And they say that it hath a singular Vertue of curing the bruised and wounded Feet of the *Pilgrims*, that stand upon it, from which it take its Name. Lastly, there are several Booths or Cabins set up, near the Shore for the *Pilgrims* to shelter themselves in from the Weather.

Having thus given a Description of the Place, I shall proceed to enquire into the Rise of *Pilgrimage* in general, and of this in particular, and then shew the great *Superstition* and *Idolatry* of it.

John Richardson
The Great Folly, Superstition, and Idolatry, of Pilgrimages in Ireland; especially of that to St. Patrick's Purgatory, 1727

Veneration of St. Patrick in Italy and Spain

The cult of St. Patrick was brought to many parts of Europe in the early middle ages by the Irish monks who laboured there. In later centuries, too, many an exile of the 17th and 18th centuries deposited in some new continental home a relic or other remembrance of Ireland's patron Saint. An exhaustive study of the present-day extent of the cult of St. Patrick across the face of Europe and of the present whereabouts of various relics etc., associated with him would be a *desideratum* of Patrician studies. Even in the past few years alone several publications have made it clear that Patrician devotion and Patrician links have lingered on in far more Continental areas than was hitherto realised in Ireland …

Italy contains a famous shrine of St. Patrick near Vertova in the province of Bergamo, the native diocese of His Holiness Pope John XXIII. Devotion to the Saint is still strong in the district and it was the scene of a historic Patrician pilgrimage of soldiers in the 1920s. Our enquiries as to whether it was the scene of any special ceremonies during the Patrician Year did not unfortunately produce any information. At least two places in Italy are named after the Irish Saint – (1) San Patrizio (a part of Conselice) in the province of Ravenna, where the parish church is also the Church of San Patrizio, and contains a picture of Ireland's apostle; (2) Torre San Patrizio in the province and diocese of Florence is dedicated to St. Patrick, and Patrician links have also come to light in Pavia and Bologna.

From the town of Torre San Patrizio the local parish priest, Don Pietro Romozzi, has kindly forwarded a summary of the history of the place and its association with St. Patrick. As early as the 11th–12th centuries the district appears under the name of *Collis Sancti Patritii* and the fortified stronghold erected there in the 13th century was called *Castrum Turris Sancti Patritii*.

A relic of St. Patrick (part of the skull) is preserved in

the Chapel of St. Patrick in the parish church, and is much venerated by the faithful. It was given to the town in 1653, and one wonders if it may not have been brought from Ireland just before that time by Rinuccini, who was of course Archbishop of Fermo. A confraternity of St. Patrick was erected with the approval of Cardinal Brancadoro, Archbishop of Fermo, in 1829, and at present numbers 45 members with a certain Michele Properzi at their head. On St. Patrick's Day annually almost all the faithful go to confession and Holy Communion, a procession is held, and several neighbouring priests take part in the ceremonies. The relic is also exposed for veneration and carried in procession at Pentecost to invoke the Saint's blessing on the crops. *'I torresi conservano la divozione verso il Santo tanto che spesso si invoca la sua protezione nelle vicissitudini della vita, si festeggia solennemente il 17 marzo con la partecipazione quasi generale ai sacramenti,'* concludes Don Romozzi's letter.

The Church of San Patrizio in Tirli possesses a 17th century altar-piece showing St. Patrick distributing Holy Communion. The annual celebration of the feast is held on 17th March and is the occasion of much popular devotion. The pastor of San Patrizio, Don Piero Manzuoli, has favoured us with a communication in which he points out that the cult of St. Patrick was introduced into that district by monks of the order of Vallombrosa, and that the church was formerly dedicated to St. Martin.

On Patrician links with Spain, Fr John Meagher of the archdiocese of Dublin, who has made a special study of Irishmen in Spain, contributes the following welcome information:

The Irish Colleges at Santiago (where there is to this day a statue of St. Patrick) and Salamanca were responsible for the introduction of the *Cultus* of St. Patrick to Northern Spain. He had already been honoured in Southern Spain since medieval times – particularly in Lorca where a victory over the Moors was attributed to his intercession.

O'Sullivan Beare by his writings on Irish history gave further impetus to his trend and interested Calderon in Saint Patrick's Purgatory in Lough Derg.

The index to the Baptismal registers in San Andres in Madrid – the registers themselves perished in the civil war – has hundreds of entries of the name *Patricio*.

In 1958 in the Cathedral of St. Peter in Jaca, Huisca (Aragon), I came across what purports to be a relic of St. Patrick. It is enclosed in a silver reliquary which also contains a relic of St. Sebastian. The relic of St. Patrick is described as *e Sabana de San Patrizio*. It is a tiny piece of cloth, and the description *Sabana* implies that it was in some way connected with the Saint personally.

How it came to Jaca is not explained in the inventories to which I had access through the kindness of the Canon Archivist, Don Juan Franciso Aznarez. As Jaca contained a large garrison and since many Irish soldiers served there is it very likely that they were responsible for its introduction to Jaca – possibly about 1727.

Anon.
Seanchas Ardmhacha: Journal of the Armagh Diocesan Society,
1961/62

St Patrick's Church in Rouen

After tracing the Irish odyssey of Saints and Earls through Brittany and Normandy in a fortnight of heady days, it was strangely like coming home to enter St. Patrick's Church in the heart of Rouen for our Pilgrimage Mass on 4 September 1978.

The imposing sculpted façade over the main doorway beckons suddenly to the visitor in the narrow street below because it strikes without warning when one turns the corner. In splendid bold relief two scenes from Patrick's life leap out to meet the eye. The upper panel depicting the miracle of the poisoned cup and the lower with its representation of the baptism of Sesgmen and his household are both encircled by cherubs in pleasing statuary ...

There was something exhilarating about the realization that this building, reconstructed about 1535, was actually standing on the site of a wooden church in honour of Patrick which predated 1228 and had been reduced to ashes by a fire which ravaged the city of Rouen in that year. One wondered with great curiosity how it could have happened that a parish in Normandy should have been dedicated to the first Archbishop of Armagh and apostle to the Irish – a parish in the heart of Rouen, a town which Patrick never visited.

Historians assure us that the Rouen of the tenth, eleventh and twelfth centuries – during the time of the dukes of Normandy – was one of the most prosperous cities in the Frankish kingdom ...

At this time the city of Rouen obtained a monopoly of trade between Normandy and Ireland ... All ships bound for Ireland, at this period, had to be fitted out at Rouen. All ships returning from Ireland were obliged to dock at Rouen once they had passed the foreland of Guernsey. Rouen imported furs from Ireland as well as hides and fish and later, in the fourteenth century, wool and cloth. The commercial links between Ireland and medieval Rouen were, in fact, so strong that Henry Plantagenet, King of England and duke of Normandy gave them royal recognition when he bestowed on the citizens of Rouen a Charter granting them a commercial monopoly with Ireland. This Charter of 1150 was ratified by Richard the Lionheart and by Philip Augustus in 1204 when Normandy reverted to the French Crown. This historical background makes it easier to imagine why it came about that a parish in Rouen was dedicated to St. Patrick. It sealed the close commercial union with Ireland which had been established and above all, it offered the Irish, who had been brought to Rouen on business, a place of worship.

We, like those bygone Irish merchants, felt beckoned by its welcome and following in the tracks of tireless tourists paused to pray and savour its atmospheric stillness.

After celebrating Mass under the shadow of a great 18th century statue of Patrick in the sanctuary we ambled around beneath the huge cylindrical columns of this boat-shaped Church. Aware that its fame in France derives from its stained glass windows (they are acknowledged to be among the finest in the entire country), the group inevitably gravitated towards the second window on the left, that of Patrick himself. Much time and imagination was then expended in the interesting and challenging task of deciphering the theme of each panel in Patrick's window. Many of the old French inscriptions are corrupted or corroded and even the scenes themselves because not generally represented pictorially in our own country, were not immediately familiar. With the help of a French text jealously guarded by the sacristan and from which some fast translation could be made, we were satisfied before leaving about all scenes depicted on this magnificent window of our national Saint. One had the strange feeling that perhaps this window tucked clandestinely in a building so very far from Ireland had preserved from the life of our national apostle enriching messages and legends which have long since slid from our own consciousness and piety.

1. The upper left hand side represents St. Patrick being baptized. A blind man sprinkles water from a spring, rising from the ground where Patrick, still a mere child, has traced the sign of the cross; the man immediately recovers his sight. At the bottom of the panel is depicted St. Patrick, who is still a youth, showing the ease with which God the Creator can intervene in the natural order, praying before a block of ice, which suddenly takes fire. An incomplete inscription reads:

'… BAPTESME SORT UNE FONTAINE … VEUX DES GLACONS …
UC …'

2. To the right, below the preceding panel we see St. Patrick,
    aged 16, kidnapped with his companions by pirates who
    bring him to Ireland. The inscription reads:

    'CEULX D'IBERNIE FONT UN EFFORT CONTRE LA BRETAGNE OU
    S.PATRIX EST PRIS PRISON …'

3. To the right, below this panel the window shows St. Patrick
    sold as a slave to an Irish prince. We see Patrick reduced to
    swineherding in the forests and on the mountains. He is
    visited by an angel of God who, from the "top of a rock"
    heralds the end of his bondage and tells him that he will find
    the sum necessary to buy his freedom, hidden in a trench
    rooted out by the swine:

    '… GARDER LES POURCEAULX SONGE … TRESOR FOUILLE PAR
    ICEULX.'

4. Below the preceding panel St. Patrick receives from Pope
    Celestine the mission of taking over as Bishop of Ireland.
    One day while resting in a house, Patrick converts the head
    of the house, together with his entire household. The son of
    this man, who received the name of Benignus in Baptism,
    and later became Bishop of Ireland on the death of Patrick
    no longer wishes to separate himself from his spiritual father,
    and with great fervour asks to be allowed follow Patrick in
    his mission.

    'RETOURNANT DE … SON HOSTE LE FILS DUQUEL CONVERTIT …'

5. Lower down, in the middle of the window is depicted
    Léogar – the most powerful of Irish kings, steeped in pagan

superstition. He unleashes all the powers of the druids on Patrick in an effort to check the rapid spread of the faith. He attempts to confine the territories won over by the holy prelate. But his efforts are in vain, since they serve only to radiate the glory which God has bestowed on his servant Patrick. When force fails Léogar resorts to trickery. He sends a poisoned drink to the bishop. Patrick calls on the name of the Lord, tilts the cup, spills the poison and makes the sign of the cross over the remainder. Then, to the amazement of those standing by, he drinks the cup and suffers no harm.

At the bottom of this tableau another incident is related. Patrick had a goat which drew the water needed for his household. One day he discovered that the beast had been stolen by an evil man, who, having eaten the goat added insult to injury by denying that he was the thief. But what should happen? From his mouth came forth a loud bleating which was heard by all (this is depicted on the window by a bright ray of glass which is inscribed 'MÉEE MÉEE'). The inscription reads:

'LE VENIN NE LUY PEUT NUIRE ET FAICT QU'UN LARON B'EELLE AINSI QUE LA BREBIS QU'IL AVAIT DEROBEE.'

Viscount Walsh, in his famous nineteenth century work *Explorations en Normandie*, records that this scene had been mistakenly believed to represent the medieval French fable 'L'Avocat Pathelin', where Patrick was taken to be Monsieur Guillaume and the thief to be Agnelet!! ...

6. On the left: one of Léogar's druids, outraged by the success of Patrick's faith, tries to provoke Patrick to work marvels in the sky. The holy bishop refuses to try the Lord God, but the druid by his craft, covers the earth with snow and overwhelms all the inhabitants with a terrifying cold. In vain the venerable bishop begs the druid to desist from his evil inclinations, but

he replies that he is incapable of retracting, since he does not have the power to undo what he has done.

Patrick replies: 'I take you at your word, and by it I must judge you. You are an evil man plunged in sorcery, a servant of Satan, you who could cause such great evil, could not do the smallest good.'

Then raising his hand he calls on the Holy Trinity, and blesses the land, and then by the power of God, the snow melts and disappears without trace.

In the same way, Patrick disperses a great darkness which the magician has caused to fall over the countryside during the daytime. The inscription reads:

'LE TEMPS NEBULEUX ET LA TERRE COUVERTE DE NEGES ET EN UN INSTANT DESCOUVERTE ET LA TERRE FERTILE.'

7. To the right of the two preceding panels we see an Irish prince by the name of Oengus being converted by the preaching of Patrick. He is baptized in the presence of his subjects. When he bows his head to receive the blessing his foot is injured by the point of Patrick's crook, but he does not feel any pain, because of the great happiness he experiences by regaining peace of soul. After the blessing the bishop sees the, wound and heals it with the sign of the cross. The inscription reads:

'MLCT SON BASTON PASTORAL POUR PRA ... ET LE PIED D'UN CAPITAINE ET LE GUERIT.'

8. In the middle of the window, on a larger scale than any of the other panels, stands the mitred figure of St. Patrick, cross in hand and wearing the pallium received from Pope Leo. At his feet appear some animals one of which seems to be a gargoyle which is normally associated with the Archbishop St. Romain, patron of Rouen. On his return from Rome, armed with many precious relics he worked

many miracles in Britain and delivered Ireland from the plague of monstrous animals whose venom brought death to all whom they touched. The inscription reads:

'IL CHASSA (D'IB) ERNIE TOUS LES BESTES.'

9. Finally, on the left, Patrick resolves to follow the examples of Moses, Elijah and Christ when he spends 40 days in the practice of penance and fasting. The panel shows him withdrawn to a high mountain where, after suffering painfully at the hands of Satan, he receives from God the privilege of seeing all the souls whom he had saved from paganism. Then, in the presence of the faithful he taps the earth with his crook. And a deep chasm opens. From this dark can be heard the moaning of people in agony. In testimony of this, the place is still called Patrick's well and purgatory: it was chosen to give a glimpse of the pain of the afterlife to a people who would not believe until they had seen. The inscription reads:

'LUY PRIANT, LA TERRE S'OUVRE QUE L'ON APELLE LE PURGATOIRE DE SAINCT PATRIX …'

The lower section of the window depicts the donors, all of whom are on their knees in prayer.

Viscount Walsh in his book tells of two other incidents: that of the leaves of the shamrock and that of the baptism of the captive birds. Unfortunately, they are no longer to be seen in this splendid window.

Gerard McGinnity
Seanchas Ardmhacha: Journal of the Armagh Diocesan Society,
1979

The Cult of St. Patrick in the Vicinity of Drackenstein

When one marks on a map the places where the cult of St. Patrick can be traced in Wuerttemberg, a group of five villages in a row in the Upper Fils Valley falls outside the main field of the cult.

At the end of a short pocket-like glen just off the upper Fils valley the parochial hamlet of Unterdrackenstein stands on a high rock, with Church, parochial house, school, mill, inn and some other buildings. In the rock of tufa stone below the church is an eleven-metre-high cave forming a hall, called in popular speech the 'Hole of the Dead', a name which points to a former cult of the Dead here …

Opposite the rock, on the other side of the narrow valley, there was formerly a large landslip with the so-called 'Dragon's Hole', from which water plunged down five metres into a large basin …

The legend relates that the dragon of 'The Dragon's Hole' kept a maiden in captivity for many years and was suitor for her favours till she was released by a youth. It is impossible to say if some beast once really made this its dwelling-place, lording the land and killing and terrifying men, who perhaps offered human sacrifice to placate it, or if the beast is merely a product of a lively imagination. In any case the centre of worship here must have been of capital significance seeing that its Christian successor was dedicated to two such mighty patrons against the dragon – the Archangel Michael, conqueror of the dragon, and the Virgin Mary …

That Michael the dragon-conqueror in statues and pictures – in Wiesensteig there is a side-altar dedicated to him – also reappears in other churches of the above-mentioned group, confirms the single religious theme of this group.

To those honoured as 'Dragon-Saints' one must add finally St. Patrick, the Irish national saint, of whom the legend relates that he drove all the snakes out of Ireland. True, only the statue of Unterdrackenstein indicates this and it is of recent date, the second half of the 19th century. It is on the lefthand side-altar, to the left of St. Sebastian, the principal figure on the altar. Patrick resembles here the usual representations in Ireland at this period. With his left hand he points downwards to a snake which lies at his feet. In Deggingen (where he is the house-patron of a farmhouse in Hofackerstrasse), Ditzenbach, Gosbach and Oberdrackenstein, a cow or sheep crouches at his feet and identifies him as the patron of livestock. He is known as such also in the principal territory in which he is honoured in Württemberg. Above all he is invoked against cattle plague, which, like the other diseases and death, came into the world through the victory of the snake over our first parents. In Hohenstadt, alone in the Württemberg district, Patrick carries a quill in his right-hand. Was it there originally or was it added during the recent restoration in order to approximate him to the four Doctors of the Church on the front of the gallery, or to the great figure of St. Gregory on the pulpit? At any rate the pen suits the author of the Confessio and the Letter to Coroticus very well.

Gertrude Mesmer
Seanchas Ardmhacha: Journal of the Armagh Diocesan Society,
  1961/62

'Patrick arrives in Saul'
St Patrick's Church, Saul

4

RELICS AND
REPRESENTATIONS

n an increasingly secular Western world, religious relics may seem anachronistic to us. In the Christian church, however, religious relics have existed since the time of Christ. No closer connection with Christ could be made than the clothes that were stripped from him at the foot of the cross; or, indeed, fragments from the true cross itself. It was always believed that reverence for the relic redounded to the honour of the saint or holy person, but by medieval times there was also an expectation of favours or benefits accruing to the devotee. St Veronica took her name from the relic she received at the crucifixion – the true image (*vera icona*) of Christ – on the cloth with which she wiped his bleeding face.

The relics of St Patrick also have that intimate connection with Jesus Christ. The most tantalising item associated with Patrick is the *Bachall Iosa* – the Staff of Christ – which was given to Patrick, as Jocelin claims in *Life and Acts of Saint Patrick*, by 'a solitary man who lived in an island in the Tuscan Sea' during his journey to Rome to be made a bishop. The reformation Archbishop of Dublin, George Browne, publicly burnt the staff in 1538 as part of his mission to clear his diocese of 'idolatry'. In researching this book it has been found that a small remnant of this staff may still exist in Ireland. What also still remain in Ireland, Italy and Spain are St Patrick's bell and its shrine; the saint's jawbone and its shrine; a fragment of his skull; and the shrine of his hand. Also, the *Domnach Airigid* – an early copy of the gospels – was once believed to have belonged to the saint.

The now traditional image of St Patrick is known across the world – the elderly episcopal figure, tall and sturdy, bearded and mitred, holding the crozier of his office in his left hand while raising his right arm in blessing, with a snake (or snakes) beneath his feet and an optional shamrock somewhere incorporated. What could be more authentic? This depiction of St Patrick first appeared in print in the seventeenth century, in a work by the Meath scholar and priest, Thomas Messingham. In 1624, Messingham published a scholarly compendium of the lives of the Irish saints – *Florilegium Insulae Sanctorum* – and included images of Saints Patrick, Bridget and Colmcille. A Tiepolo altarpiece in the Museo Civico in Padua, previously believed to represent St Paulinus of Aquileia, has now been accepted as representing St Patrick because of the 1985 detective work of Catherine Whistler. This Italian masterpiece indicates the spread of the cult of Saint Patrick throughout Europe.

The ninth-century representation of two clerical persons on the north side of the cross of Saints Patrick and Columba in Kells, is possibly the earliest representation of the saint. What may surprise the reader is the fact that no popularly recognisable image or representation of the saint existed before the seventeenth century, twelve hundred years after his death. This inevitably gave rise to speculation as to the features of the saint, his height and build, whether and how he was tonsured; even as to whether he was bearded or shaven.

Since the seventeenth century, then, artists have been given free rein in their representation of St Patrick; a circumstance which has enriched the world of portraiture, statuary, stained glass and mosaic.

The Relics of Saint Patrick:
A photographic feature with notes on the relics

The custom of enshrining the relics of saints was established at a very early date in Irish ecclesiastical practice. The earliest reliquaries were probably simple little caskets to contain objects associated with a saint, or else larger stone shrines to contain bones. But at least as early as the eighth century the custom had begun of making reliquaries which took their shape from that of the object enshrined – staff, bell, book etc.

There must have been many churches in the country which claimed to hold relics of St. Patrick. No doubt some of these were authentic and some were not, but there is no object whose history we can document back to the fifth century. The earliest reference we have to relics of St. Patrick is that transcribed by the early mediaeval compiler of the Annals of Ulster from the lost 'Book of Cuanu' in his entry under the year 552:

> I found it written in the Book of Cuanu that the relics of Patrick were enshrined sixty years after Patrick's death by Colmcille. Three valuable relics were found in the tomb, the chalice, the Gospel of the Angel and the Bell of the Will. This is how the angel gave the three relics to Colmcille, the chalice to Down, the Bell of the Will to Armagh and the Gospel of the Angel to Colmcille himself. It is called the Gospel of the Angel because Colmcille received it from the Angel's hand.

There is another reference to the opening of the grave of St. Patrick which is worth quoting because it was written at the beginning of the eighth century. It is in Tirechan's memoir and it reads:

> Colmcille at the inspiration of the Holy Spirit, opened the tomb of Patrick, proving that it is in Saul of Patrick, that is, in the church beside the sea.

These are the earliest references to relics of St. Patrick. They do not include a mention of the Staff of Jesus, *Bachall Iosa,* regarded throughout the Middle Ages as one of the chief relics, which was destroyed in Dublin at the time of the reformation. The shrines and relics described here are associated in tradition with St. Patrick, but their actual connection with the Saint is in most cases impossible to establish.

The Book of Armagh

The Book of Armagh now preserved in the library of Trinity College, Dublin, is the most important historical manuscript of Ireland prior to the 12th century. It is a small volume (approximately 7" by 5") consisting of 222 leaves of vellum and it contains three main divisions: (1) Documents relating to St. Patrick (including the Confessio, Tirechan and Muirchu), ff. 1–24; (2) The New Testament, ff. 25–190; (3) The Life of St. Martin of Tours by Sulpicius Severus, ff. 192–222. It is probable that originally several of the divisions of the book were separate codices.

From inscriptions in the book it is known to have been written by Ferdomnach, a scribe of Armagh, at the dictation of Torbach who was abbot of Armagh for a short period in 807 and 808. An entry in the Annals of the Four Masters under 937 refers to a *cumhdach* [reliquary or covering] (now lost) being provided for the Book of Armagh. In 1004 Brian Boroimhe visited Armagh and had entered in the manuscript a confirmation of the privileges claimed by the clergy of that church. At some unknown date the manuscript went into the keeping of a family who took the name Mac Maoir or Mac Moyre from their stewardship of the book, and it remained in their possession until 1680. It came up for sale in 1853 and was purchased by Dr. William Reeves who presented it to Trinity College Library in the following year.

The second section of the book after the Patrician

documents contains the only manuscript copy of the complete New Testament of Irish origin. The gospels are enhanced with elegant pen-drawings but colour is completely absent. The symbols of the Evangelists are particularly striking and original and the animal ornament is close in character and probably influenced by the style of the Book of Kells. The style of the ornament agrees with the date given by the inscription.

The Satchel of the Book

The leather satchel of the Book of Armagh is also preserved in Trinity College Library. It is decorated with panels of interlacing and animal ornament. It was not made for the book and is of late mediaeval date.

The Bell of St. Patrick's Will

The bell is a quadrilateral iron bell (approximately 7" high and 5" wide) made from two plates of iron which were bent and riveted together. Subsequently the whole bell was dipped in bronze. The handle is of iron let into the top of the bell. The clapper which is probably later is also of iron. This is the ordinary lay cow-bell type of bell, but it is possibly the original bell of St. Patrick which was mentioned in the Annals of Ulster at A.D. 552, where it is referred to as *'clocc in oidheachta'*. Since the bell was enshrined in the late 11th century its history is known.

The Shrine of the Bell

The elaborately ornamented shrine is made of bronze adorned in the front with silver-gilt plates and elaborate filigree patterns of animal interlacings. The rather crude settings of rock-crystal were probably added later. The back is decorated with an openwork diaper pattern of crosses and a half-uncial inscription runs round its plain marginal border. Both sides have openwork interlace ornament. The crest has, at the back, a pair of peacocks symmetrically opposed, a version of the well-known 'well-of-life' pattern, and above them more zoomorphic interlace. The front of the crest is rather similar but has patterns of filigree instead of the peacocks. The inscription in Irish half-uncials reads:

OR DO DOMNALL U LACHLAIND LASINDERNAD IN CLOC SA
OCUS DO DOMNALL CHOMARBA PHATRAIC ICONDERNAD
OCUS DOD CHATHALAN U MAELCHALLAND DO MAER IN
CHLUIC OCUS DO CHONDUILIG U INMAINEN CONA MACCAIB
RO CUMTAIG

Translation of inscription and relevant dates

A prayer for Domnall O Lachlaind (king of Ireland 1083–1121) under whose auspices this bell was made. And for Domnall, successor of Patrick (abbot of Armagh 1091–1105), in whose house it was made. And for Cathalan O Mael-Challand, steward of the bell. And for Cu Duilig O Inmainen and his sons who covered it.

This shows that the shrine was made, probably at Armagh, between 1091 and 1105. It remained in the hands of its keepers, the O Mulhollands, a family who were located in Co. Tyrone and later in Co. Derry (except for a period when it was held by the O'Mellans) until 1758 when the last keeper died. His grandson left it to a Mr. Adam Mac Clean of Belfast and it passed from his executors to Dr. Todd and then to the Collections of the Royal Irish Academy now in the National Museum.

This bell-shrine is one of the most splendid objects of Early Christian Irish art. The zoomorphic interlace is in the Irish Urnes style which appears also on the Cross of Cong and St. Manchan's Shrine. The technique of the openwork animal patterns is unusual as all the separate elements of the design are soldered together. The filigree work is exceedingly elaborately executed.

The 'Fiacail Phadruig' or Shrine of St. Patrick's Tooth

This is a purse-shaped wooden case (11" by 9") covered with bronze and silver and ornamented with figures in relief, filigree work and settings of crystal, glass and amber. It is said traditionally to have been made to contain one of St. Patrick's teeth. The upper

portion has an openwork crest of foliage pattern above a series of pointed arches. The front has an ornamented cross-bar with a crystal setting above which is a crucifixion and below a figure of St. Patrick. Other saints represented include St. Benon, St. Brendan and St. Columcille (St Brigid is named but is missing) and the four Evangelists.

The back is divided into four panels by a cruciform mounting and the divisions contain engraved figures of ecclesiastics. There are bands of gold and silver filigree on both front and back.

On the front cross-bar is a Latin inscription which states that 'Thomas de Bramighen, Lord of Athenry, caused me to be ornamented in this part.' Thomas de Birmingham died in A.D. 1376 and the character of much of the ornament is consistent with a 14th century date. The shrine has been much damaged and repaired and portion of the ornament is probably somewhat earlier than the inscription.

In tradition the Fiacail Phadruig is related to the church of Killaspugbrone, Co. Sligo, where St. Patrick is said to have lost a tooth. Its earlier history is unknown but in the early 19th century a man named Reilly was going about the west of Ireland with it performing cures. It was rescued from him by the Abbot of the Augustinian Canons of Cong and afterwards was preserved at Blake Hill near Cong and at Mionnloch Castle. From there it was given to Dr. Stokes who deposited it in the collections of the Royal Irish Academy.

The Shrine of St. Patrick's Hand

This shrine now belongs to the Bishop of Down and Connor. It is a case of silver 15½" long and represents the hand and arm of an ecclesiastic covered by an embroidered and jewelled sleeve. The fingers are in the position of episcopal blessing. There is no definite evidence that the shrine contained any relic of St. Patrick but it is traditionally said to have come from the high altar of Down Cathedral where it had been placed containing the arm of the saint. It was kept first by the Magennis family and afterwards by the Russells, Nugents and Mc Henrys. The last-named family transferred it to the Most Rev. Dr. Denvir, Bishop of Down and Connor in 1840. The style of the shrine is consistent with a fifteenth century date.

The Black Bell of St. Patrick

This is a mere fragment of an iron bell which came originally from the parish of Killower near Headford, Co. Galway. In one of the ancient descriptions of the hereditary property of the O'Flahertys it is said that "Mac Beolan of Killower is the keeper of the black bell of St. Patrick.' In the 19th century it was in the possession of the Gerarty family near Ballinrobe who brought it every year to the pattern on Croagh Patrick. It was procured from them by Sir William Wilde and given to the Academy Collections, now in the National Museum.

The Shrine of St. Patrick's Jaw

This shrine consists of a silver box enclosing a human jawbone and roughly shaped to suit it. In 1854 it was in the possession of the Cullen family at Castle Robin near Lisburn, Co. Antrim. At that time one double tooth remained in the jaw and others had been removed and given to members of the family who had emigrated. The tradition in the family, who had held the shrine for generations, was that it was the jaw-bone of St. Patrick. The silver case was said to be embossed in 19th century style but had apparently a hall-mark of earlier date. The present location of this shrine is St. Malachy's College, Belfast.

The main decorative element on it is a skull and cross-bones on the top. The shrine varies from 5¼" to 4¾" in width at the top and is about 4½" long at the bottom. Its height varies from 2¾" to 1¾".

St. Patrick's Protection

Lassar gréne áne,
apstal Hérenn hóge,
Pátraic co méit míle
rop dítiu ar tróge.

The flame of a splendid sun,
The apostle of virginal Erin,
May Patrick with many thousands
Be the shelter of our wretchedness.

from *Félire Oengusso* (c. 800 A.D.)

Dr. Máire De Paor
Seanchas Ardmhacha: Journal of the Armagh Diocesan Society,
    1961/62

Domnach Airgid

Named after the shrine (the 'Silver Church') in which it was found at Clones in County Monaghan, this small fragment of St Matthew's Gospel has become associated with the story of St Patrick's presentation of a gospel book to St Macartan at

the time of his appointment to the See of Clogher. The older part of the shrine belongs to the eighth century, but the Gospel fragment itself is a good deal older than that. Some date it to the late fifth or early sixth century.

Public Record Office Ireland

Michael Slavin
The Ancient Books of Ireland, 2005

How in His Journey to Rome
He Found the Staff of Jesus

And being desirous that his journey and all his acts should by the apostolic authority be sanctioned, he was earnest to travel unto the city of Saint Peter, and there more thoroughly to learn the canonical institutes of the holy Roman Church. And when he had unfolded his purpose unto Germanus, the blessed man approved thereof, and associated unto him that servant of Christ, Sergecius the presbyter, as the companion of his journey, the solace of his labor, and the becoming testimony of his holy conversation. Proceeding, therefore, by the divine impulse, or by the angelic revelation, he went out of his course unto a solitary man who lived in an island in the Tuscan Sea; and the solitary man was pure in his life, and he was of great desert and esteemed of all, and in his name and in his works he was Just; and after their holy greetings were passed, this man of God gave unto Patrick a staff which he declared himself to have received from the hands of the Lord Jesus.

And there were in this island certain other solitary men, who lived apart from him, some of whom appeared to be youths, and other decrepit old men, with whom when Patrick had conversed, he learned that the oldest of them were the sons of the youths; and when St. Patrick, marveling, enquired of them the cause of so strange a miracle, they answered unto him, saying: 'We from our childhood were continually intent on works of charity, and our door was open to every traveller who asked for victual or for lodging in the name of Christ, when on a certain night we received a stranger having in his hand a staff; and we showed unto him so much kindness as we could, and in the morning he blessed us, and said, I am Jesus Christ, unto whose members ye have hitherto ministered, and whom ye have last night entertained in His own person. Then the staff which He bore in His hand gave He unto yonder man of God, our spiritual father, commanding him that he should preserve it safely, and deliver it unto a certain stranger named Patrick, who would, after many days were passed, come unto him. Thus saying, He ascended into heaven; and ever since we have continued in the same youthful state, but our sons, who were then infants, have, as thou seest, become decrepit old men.'

And Patrick, giving thanks unto God, abided with the man of God certain days, profiting in God by his example yet more and more; at length he bade him farewell, and went on his way with the staff of Jesus, which the solitary man had proffered unto him. O excellent gift! descending from the Father of light, eminent blessing, relief of the sick, worker of miracles, mercy sent of God, support of the weary, protection of the traveller! For as the Lord did many miracles by the rod in the hand of Moses, leading forth the people of the Hebrews out of the land of Egypt, so by the staff that had been formed for His own hands was He pleased, through Patrick, to do many and great wonders to the conversion of many nations. And the staff is held in much veneration in Ireland, and even unto this day it is called the staff of Jesus.

Jocelin
Life and Acts of Saint Patrick
Translated by Edmund L. Swift
The Most Ancient Lives of Saint Patrick, 1874

The Burning of the Bachall Iosa

In 1535, Henry sent to Dublin as Archbishop of that See George Browne, the ex-Augustinian English friar, who rivalled his royal master in anti-Catholic zeal. The next year, 1536, Browne caused to be passed in the 'Irish' parliament a bill, investing the King with the ownership of all the monasteries in Ireland with a view to their suppression. This necessitated a commission being set up, so that the actual work of suppression did not begin till 1539. Browne, meantime, had actively begun to clear his archdiocese of 'idolatry', and in 1538 he publicly burned the Bachall Iosa, the crozier which for eleven centuries had been preserved and venerated as being the actual crozier carried about by St. Patrick on his missionary journeys.

Henry Morris
'The Iconography of St. Patrick'
Down and Connor Historical Society's Journal, 1936

The Crozier of Rev. Dr Slattery

The crozier of most Rev. Dr Slattery, in the shaft of which is enclosed a small portion of the wood of the staff of St Patrick, and a fragment of the shrine in which it was encased. On the shaft there is an inscription to the effect that the particle of the staff of the saint was given to the Archbishop Dr Slattery by the O'Kearney 'Crux' family, in whose possession it had been for centuries, and that he had it inserted in his crozier in 1848.

Catalogue entry
In the care of the Archdiocese of Cashel & Emly

Archdiocese of Cashel & Emly

The Altar Stone of Saul Abbey

The Altar stone on which St. Patrick is said to have celebrated Holy Communion is now in the Roman Catholic Church at Saul. It is ten feet long, five inches thick and four feet three inches broad, but unfortunately broken. It was once the High Altar of Saul Abbey. When the Abbey was in ruins a certain man wished to make the huge stone the door-step for a new house he was building at the junction of Saul Street and Scotch Street in Downpatrick in the year 1757. So he sent a wagon drawn by oxen to Saul to carry the stone but the oxen were very upset, the wagon turned over at the top of Saul Hill and the stone broke. Later misfortune overtook the man who had attempted this sacrilege.

The Altar stone was carried from the hill on which it lay to Saul Chapel after its erection in 1782 and thence to the subsequent new church.

Maureen Donnelly
Saint Patrick and the Downpatrick Area, 1981

Diocese of Down and Connor

Silver reliquary bust

A silver reliquary bust of Saint Patrick. The piece consists of a tonsured head, made in France, with a hinged top. There is an oval grille in the top of the head to allow the relic to be seen. The head is placed on an octagonal base with quatrefoil decoration: this was made in Ireland and is inset with nine crystals. The piece is supported by seven crouching lions. There is an inscription around the bust which reads: *Dominus Jacobus Butler Iarius/Iarins Comes De Ormond Justiciar Ins Hibernie Hoc Opus Fieri Fecit Ad Honorem Sancti Patricii* [Lord James Butler, Earl of Ormond, Justiciar of the island of Ireland, had me made in honour of St Patrick]. French and Irish.

Hunt Museum

The Hunt Museum, Limerick

The Shrine of St. Patrick's Hand

The shrine of St Patrick's Hand, the only arm-reliquary of Gothic form in Ireland, has recently been deposited in the Ulster Museum on long-term loan by the Diocese of Down and Connor. Here, Cormac Bourke, Assistant Keeper of Antiquities at the Ulster Museum, Belfast, gives a preliminary account of the shrine in advance of full publication.

The enshrinement of the relics of saints was commonplace from the early centuries of Christianity and was practised with great zeal during the Middle Ages. Relics were defined as objects which had touched the body of a saint, the corporeal remains themselves and articles used by the saint in life. In Ireland and northern Britain corporeal relics, after initial burial below ground, were sometimes placed in free-standing shrines of stone, a reflex of the Classical sarcophagus or mortuary house. It became customary to place such relics either in small quantities in portable tomb-shaped shrines of wood and metal, or singly in containers which reflected, more or less, the shape of the relic within. Objects associated with the saint's life were similarly treated. Thus bell-shrines and book-shrines are relatively numerous; there is one surviving belt-shrine and some evidence that others existed.

The practice of enshrinement was pious in origin but acquired political and economic aspects. A church rich in relics became a focus of pilgrimage and could claim primacy over its fellows. In Ireland relics could be used directly to raise revenue and were the basis of the authority under which some ecclesiastical law was enacted and enforced. It is not surprising that elaborate shrines were made to hold and transport the relics upon which so much depended. This elevation of the material remains of saints had its written counterpart in hagiography. An index of the influence and well-being of a church was the strength of the cult of its founder, and such cults were based in equal measure on written Lives and on the material relics of the saints.

The most developed cult of medieval Ireland was that of Patrick, the fifth-century patron saint. His remains were said to have been enshrined by Columba in 553, and there is a record of their re-discovery and translation into Downpatrick Cathedral in 1185–86. An iron hand-bell attributed to Patrick was enshrined in the period 1091–1105, although it is unlikely in the extreme that the bell belonged to the saint or is as old as the fifth century. The Book of Armagh, which contains several

Patrician texts, was viewed with similar reverence and enshrined in 937, although in fact the manuscript is of ninth-century date.

Another relic was the *Bachall Isu*, a crozier attributed to Patrick, which was destroyed in Dublin during the Reformation. The *Fiacail Phádraig*, or Shrine of St Patrick's Tooth, is a bag-shaped reliquary reputedly made for a tooth of Patrick preserved at Killaspugbrone, Co. Sligo. Of post-medieval date is the Shrine of St Patrick's Jaw, a silver box containing a human lower jaw-bone which belongs to the diocese of Down and Connor. The Shrine of St Patrick's Hand, a Gothic arm-reliquary from Co. Down, belongs to the same diocese. This shrine, which is unique in Ireland, has recently been deposited on long-term loan in the Department of Antiquities of the Ulster Museum.

Despite its importance, the early history of the reliquary is obscure. The first published account appeared in 1847 and gives a history of the shrine derived from Father James McAleenan, parish priest of Portaferry in the Ards peninsula. This account associates the shrine with the translation of the relics of Patrick into Down Cathedral in 1186 and records its removal by Edward Bruce in 1316. After Bruce's defeat at Faughart in 1318 the shrine is said to have passed to the Magennis family of south Co. Down, with whom it remained until the early eighteenth century, thereafter passing to the Savage/Nugent family of Portaferry, one of whom gave it later in the eighteenth century to the local parish priest. After his death it came into the possession of the McHenrys of Carrstown, south of Portaferry, who retained it until about 1840, when it was acquired by Bishop Denvir for the Diocese of Down and Connor.

The earlier part of this account is open to question. There is in fact no evidence that the shrine was made in 1186 or that it was among the objects stolen in 1316. Father McAleenan's account should be compared with that of Mrs Crangle of Carrstown, quoted by O'Laverty [author of *An Historical Account of the Diocese of Down and Connor*, 1895], which records only that 'when Down Cathedral was plundered, Magennis saved the reliquary', adding a description of its later history which agrees broadly with that of 1847. This less learned tradition of the shrine reinforces the link with the Magennises but omits reference to the events of 1186 and 1316. As we shall see, the shrine is of fourteenth or fifteenth century date. If, as seems likely, it derives from Downpatrick, the shrine could have been retained by the Magennises at the Dissolution, when members of that family were respectively bishop and archdeacon of Down. The plundering mentioned in Mrs Crangle's account may refer to the burning of the Cathedral in 1538 by Lord Deputy Grey.

The shrine, which is entirely hollow and made of gilt silver, is a naturalistic representation of a sleeved right forearm and hand in the attitude of benediction. The forearm is made of two pieces of sheet metal, each closed to a roughly conical shape, in which diagonal ridges represent the folds of drapery. The two parts are graded in size and the lower overlaps the upper in a simple diagonal joint which lies parallel to the folds. On the back of the sleeve a die-stamped panel, applied at the lower margin, bears a single pattern of animal ornament in two registers, and the same pattern in one register decorates a narrower panel at the cuff. The upper edge of the latter is overlapped by an alternating series of three large and four small domed studs. All have been identified scientifically as glass; the large studs are light green in colour and of the others three are black and one is dark blue. The lower panel

NMNI

163

is partly concealed by five oval studs, one of rock crystal and the other four of clear glass. Both panels are framed in twisted wire, and the same wire delimits two fields on the front of the sleeve which correspond to those filled by the panels on the back. These fields were probably once occupied by further die-stamped panels.

The junction of sleeve and hand is effected where the basal edge of a *fleur-de-lis* strip and that of the wrist which it encloses are soldered to the edges of two sections of tubing, one within the other, which are concealed beneath the upper portion of the sleeve. This arrangement appears to be recent and is probably the work of John Donegan, the Dublin watchmaker and silversmith, who repaired the shrine for Bishop Denvir in the nineteenth century. In the original arrangement the upper sleeve may have enclosed a tubular extension of the wrist.

The body of the hand was made as a unit to which the thumb was attached by soldering. The fingers are simple tubes which are inserted into the body of the hand and project visibly internally. The distal ends of the little finger and third finger, which are flexed, were made separately and attached to the proximal ends by soldering. The fingers and thumb are each capped or closed by an applied oval plate and all the nails are indicated. A ring is soldered in position on the second finger; the bezel is set with a stud of light purple glass (seemingly a restoration) and a small gap interrupts the back of the hoop. The hand is otherwise bare and there is no truth in the suggestion, repeated in the literature, that it wears a jewelled glove. A shallow oblong depression in the back of the hand is outlined in twisted wire and covered by a framed and hinged lid of rock crystal. A longitudinal incision in the metal which allowed the depression to be created has been revealed by X-ray, although concealed beneath a modern lining.

The shrine of St Patrick's Hand belongs to a type of reliquary which was standardized in western Europe between the twelfth and the seventeenth centuries. The earliest known example, the arm-reliquary of St Blaise in Brunswick Cathedral, is of late eleventh-century date. The only other Irish specimen, the Shrine of St Lachtin's Arm, dates to the early twelfth century and is unique in the entire series in that all the fingers are flexed. In every other instance, the fingers and thumb are either fully extended, are in the attitude of benediction or hold a saintly attribute.

With a small number of exceptions, arm-reliquaries are made of metal and consist of a sleeved forearm and hand, with or without a wooden core. In some cases the hand is represented as gloved and from the fourteenth century many were provided with rings. Either the right or left forearm and hand can be represented and two reliquaries sometimes form a matching pair. Both single- and double-sleeved reliquaries are known. The sleeves are usually rendered realistically, although many of the single-sleeved type (to which the Shrine of St Lachtin's Arm belongs) have a smooth, if patterned, surface. In double-sleeved reliquaries the 'inner' sleeve in fact extends only from the cuff of the 'outer' sleeve to the wrist. The Shrine of St Patrick's Hand is of this type, although highly unusual in that a border alone represents the inner sleeve.

While its overall form places the Shrine of St Patrick's Hand in the mainstream of the European series, its place and date of manufacture can be established only by a consideration of its ornament, specifically the die-stamped panels on the sleeve and the *fleur-de-lis* border at the wrist. The die-stamped panels repeat three times a single pattern which consists (reading from left to right) of two confronted lions, two confronted griffins and two confronted stags. The panel at the cuff bears in addition the remains of a bird, facing right, at the extreme right-hand end.

These animals and a number of others were derived from illustrated bestiaries and are characteristic of Irish art of the late Middle Ages, surviving chiefly in the durable media of metal and stone. In metal, such animals often appear, as on the Shrine of St Patrick's hand, in die-stamped panels. These are thin pieces of foil on which ornament is reproduced in relief by stamping with a die in which the pattern is cut in intaglio. As a rule in Irish metalwork two animals of different species form confronted pairs, e.g. on the *Corp Naomh* and the *Cathach* (dragon v lion), and the *Bearnan Chonaill* (griffin v lion). The animals on the Shrine of St Patrick's Hand compare in detail with those on the *Corp Naomh* and the *Cathach*, which are of fourteenth- or fifteenth-century date, although on St Patrick's Hand animals of a single species form confronted pairs. A parallel is provided by a bronze die, now lost, from Doohatty, Co. Monaghan, which bore a pattern of identical birds in confronted pairs.

The die-stamped panels on the shrine demonstrate that it is of Irish origin and of fourteenth- or fifteenth-century date. The panels themselves are clearly original; like the sleeve they are of gilt silver and their presence was anticipated by the designer. The lower margin of the sleeve beneath the extant panel bears a series of triangular cuts which allowed a consistent flaring of the sleeve, but which are visible only internally and which the panel effectively conceals. The studs of green, black and blue glass on the cuff are likewise original and are consistent with a fourteenth- or fifteenth-century date. A similar light green glass was employed in the fourteenth-century phase of the Shrine of the Stowe Missal and in roughly contemporary additions to the back of the *Fiacail Phádraig*.

One of the large studs at the lower end of the sleeve is rock crystal and the other four are clear glass. The latter can be attributed to John Donegan, who is known to have replaced some missing 'Irish diamonds' in the nineteenth century. Those he replaced, together with the surviving rock crystal stud, were probably primary, since such studs appear in much ecclesiastical metalwork of the period. Equally typical of the age is the open-work *fleur-de-lis* border at the wrist, which compares with such borders on Gothic crucifixes of the fifteenth century, several of which are known from Ireland.

Thus the detailing of the Shrine of St Patrick's Hand declares it to be an Irish exemplar of a European type. Two further aspects of the shrine reinforce its Insular character. Only one Continental arm-reliquary, that of San Domingo de Silos, is similarly provided with an opening in the back of the hand. This feature, designed to render the relic visible, is usually sited in the sleeve. In the Shrine of St Patrick's Hand the opening gives access only to a small cavity which functioned independently of the sleeve, and which until recently housed a relic obtained in the last century in Rome. O'Laverty records that when the sleeve was opened in 1856 it contained a piece of yew wood 'about nine inches long ... bored lengthwise with a hole sufficiently large to receive the wrist bone of a human arm' and that 'the wood was smeared over at both ends with wax'. No trace of the bone remained in 1856 and the wooden receptacle itself has since disappeared. However, there is no reason to doubt that it was a primary feature of the shrine and among medieval Irish craftsmen yew was a favoured wood. The lesser cavity too is apparently original, being lidded with rock crystal and not glass. That the popular name of the reliquary fails to reflect its principal purpose, namely to enshrine an *arm*, may be due to the prominence of the opening in the hand. The provision of two cavities is not unique, for a reliquary in Trier contains relics in the sleeve and in the thumb. While the wooden component in the Irish shrine may have housed the principal relic it cannot be described as a *core*, since the shrine is structurally stable without it. However, the possibility remains that the resetting of the hand carried out by Donegan was necessitated by its loss.

The Insular character of the Shrine of St Patrick's Hand is underlined, secondly, by the absence of a raised base or plinth, a standard feature of the Continental series after the thirteenth century. The base is a flat plate with a central concavity bearing the IHS monogram in Roman capitals, although either Lombardic or Gothic lettering should be expected. Roman lettering was probably adopted in Ireland in the sixteenth century, the date of its appearance in the late medieval crosses of Meath. Thus the lettering on the base may be secondary to the original plate, if the plate itself is not secondary to the shrine. It is thus possible, though unlikely, that a raised plinth once existed.

The Shrine of St Patrick's Hand is not a *tour-de-force* of metal-working. The joint in the sleeve is crudely effected and the capping of the fingers and thumb has little semblance of naturalism. A lack of imagination is evident in the choice of die-stamped panels, which repeat the same pattern three times. Despite this, the shrine is visually arresting and in aesthetic terms is greater than the sum of its parts.

The shrine can only have been commissioned by a major church and in honour of a major saint. Although we lack a contemporary record of its production, in the absence of any evidence to the contrary it is probable that the saint was Patrick and that the church was the cathedral church of Down.

Cormac Bourke
Irish Arts Review, 1987

The Jaw-bone of Saint Patrick

It is in this area of the Savage family of Drumaroad and the Franciscans of Drumnaquoile that we first hear mention specifically of another relic, 'the Jaw-bone of Saint Patrick'.

Pat Foy also mentions the Savage Family of Drumaroad. He recounts a story of Priest-hunting in this area of Down and how the names of certain protestant families are still remembered for the kindness they showed to hunted priests. One of the fire-side stories of Lecale relates how a captured priest was taken to the home of Jocelyn Hamilton and locked in a room to be conveyed to Downpatrick the next morning. Hamilton, however, directed one of his Catholic servants to saddle his horse and take the priest, during the night, to the home of Mr. Savage, a 'well known Catholic in Drumaroad'. The escape caused a good deal of consternation, and Hamilton's cousin, Sheriff Bernard Ward, chastised him for conniving at the priest's escape. It is said that both later died at each other's hands in a dual.

The mountainous area of Drumaroad and Drumnaquoile had truly become a 'locus refugii', a 'place of refuge' for the friars. Down and Connor had no Bishop for twenty years. In 1671, Dr Daniel Mackey was appointed, residing at Slieveaniskey in the same area. He died two years later at a time of renewed persecution. In a letter announcing his death, Saint Oliver Plunkett wrote;

> On the vigil of Christmas, Monsignor Daniel Mackey, the Bishop of Down and Connor, most perfectly obeyed the last edict and departed not only from Ireland, but from the world, to enjoy, as we hope, a country and a kingdom where he will be free from the parliament of England and its edicts ... At his death he had no more than eighteen pence, so that to have a private funeral it may be necessary to sell part of his goods.

Fr Park tells us that a reliquary once hung above the altar of the old chapel of Drumaroad, which had originally belonged to the Franciscan Friary. It is described as 'gilded, and closed with a double door'. It was removed at the rebuilding in 1838 and now seems to be lost.

In September 1951 Canon Cahill of Drumaroad and Clanvaraghan inaugurated a memorial cross in stone at Drumnaquoile to commemorate the Franciscan presence.

Taking into account the area of the 'locus refugii' of the Franciscan friars, originally from Downpatrick, and the fact that a family called Savage, a name already connected to Patrician relics, also lived and had their homestead there, is it all that surprising that the first mention of a relic called 'The Jaw-bone of Saint Patrick' should emerge from there?

Monsignor James O'Laverty relates how this relic passed originally from a family called Savage of Dunturk, Seaforde, Co. Down, an area not far from Drumaroad, Drunmaquoile and Slieveanisky ...

Continuing his account, O'Laverty relates how the relic came to Derriaghy;

> The Most Rev. Dr Dorrian has also a silver reliquary, which he purchased from a family named Cullen, who resided in the Parish of Derriaghy, Co. Antrim, at the base of Colin Mountain. It consists of a silver box, or shrine enclosing a human jaw-bone, in a perfect state, but now only retaining one double tooth. It had formerly five, three of which were given to members of the family when emigrating to America, and the fourth was deposited under the altar of Derriaghy Chapel by the parish priest, when the Chapel was rebuilt in 1797. The outer case is of antique appearance, fitted with a lid, and has a hall-mark of some early date impressed upon it. The bone is that of a male of rather a large size. The family believed that it was the jaw-bone of Saint Patrick, and a tradition to that effect has been handed down for generations. The great grandmother of the old men, the Cullens, who sold it to the Bishop, bought it from her relations, the Savages of Dunturk, in the county of Down. Formerly water, in which the bone was immersed, was administered to persons afflicted with epilepsy.

O'Laverty again mentions this relic under 'his entry for 'Derriaghy Chapel';

Derriaghy Chapel was again rebuilt in 1802, by Fr John Devlin, who was then curate to Fr O'Donnell (Parish Priest of Derriaghy, Belfast and Drum, and later first Parish Priest of Belfast) … It was later dedicated under the invocation of Saint Patrick and a portion of the relic of Saint Patrick, which had long been preserved in the parish, in a silver shrine, by a family named Cullen was placed in the altar.

Dean Brendan McGee, presently serving in St Patrick's Parish, Donegall Street, Belfast has played an important role in the preservation of the history of the Parish of Derriaghy, where he served as curate for many years (1950s). He believes that the home of the Cullen family, keepers of the relic, is the house owned in recent times, by the Burns family. This house, on the Belsize Road (at the top of the Moss Road, Lambeg), was recently rebuilt. The family run the Cribstown Garden Centre. In the old house the Burns family had a tradition that a penal chalice had once been hidden in a niche beside the fire place. Might this be a corrupted memory of a hiding place for a relic?

But Dr Máire de Paor places the Cullen family at Castle Robin, higher up the mountain, on the border of the presently constituted Parish of Derriaghy.

In an article in the 'Seanchas Ardmhacha' of the Patrician year of 1961 she describes the shrine and relic:

The shrine consists of a silver box enclosing a human jaw-bone and roughly shaped to suit it. In 1854 it was in the possession of the Cullen family at Castle Robin near Lisburn, Co. Antrim. At that time one double tooth remained in the jaw and others had been removed and given to members of the family who had emigrated. The tradition in the family, who had held the shrine for generations, was that it was the jaw-bone of Saint Patrick. The silver case is said to be embossed in nineteenth century style but had apparently a hall-mark of an earlier date. The present location of the shrine is in St Malachy's College, Belfast.

The main decorative element on it is a skull and crossbones on the top. The shrine varies from 5¼" to 4¾" in the width at the top and is about 4½" long at the bottom. Its height varies from 2¾" to 1¾".

Included in the 'Seanchas Ardmhacha' of 1961 are four photographs, three of the shrine of the relic and one of the jaw-bone itself. The plate of photos is undated. This is intriguing, as for much of the nineteenth and the twentieth centuries, at least within the diocese of Down and Connor itself, the shrine and relic seemed lost and generally forgotten. Fr Leo McKeown, Parish Priest of Newtownards, wrote a pamphlet for the Patrician events in 1961. He mentions the relics of Patrick, which were in evidence on these occasions, the 'Bell of Saint Patrick' and the 'Annals of Ulster', but not the jaw-bone. Monsignor Joseph Maguire, late Parish Priest of Downpatrick, formerly Parish Priest of Drumaroad and Clanvaraghan, and one-time teacher in Saint Malachy's College, Belfast, created an impressive new memorial to the Saint in his extension of Saint Patrick's Church, Downpatrick.

However the author has found six different references elsewhere to the shrine and relic. No doubt other references also exist.

The first mention, after the disappearance of the relic from the Parish of Derriaghy, is to be found in the *Ulster Journal of Archaeology* in 1854.

The second reference is actually a summary of the article in the *Ulster Journal of Archaeology* of 1854, by D. MacSioduin, hand-written and placed like a scroll into the 'Shrine of the Jaw-bone' in 1919. It seems likely that MacSioduin was attached to Saint Malachy's College. 'The note he enclosed is mostly a repetition of the account given by O'Laverty, already mentioned. He only adds that "the case is … rather fancifully embossed …

It is held in high veneration …" (water in which it was immersed) was also used as an antidote for all cattle diseases. Whenever this bone is lifted out of the shrine a towel or handkerchief is used to prevent contamination by the hand.'

In 1946 we come across a third reference by Cathal O'Byrne:

> Stories told of fearful visitations of providence which befell those who burned their humble Church. Until Derriaghy Church was again rebuilt in 1802, Mass was said in a barn belonging to Michael O'Kane at the White Mountain. The church built then was however half the size of that which had been (re)-built in 1749. It was dedicated to Saint Patrick, and a portion of the relic of the saint, which had long been preserved in the parish in a silver shrine by a family named Cullen, was placed in the altar.

The fourth mention I have come across concerns Fr Sean Cahill, Parish Priest of Castlewellan (Kilmegan) and his uncle, Canon Cahill (already mentioned), Parish Priest of Drumaroad and Clanvaraghan. When Fr Sean Cahill was a 'Queensman' (a Seminarian) in 'The Wing', St Malachy's College, Belfast, he remembers his uncle, in the 1950s, telling him about the local tradition of the relic and the Savage family, but the Canon did not seem to know the relic resided in St Malachy's College.

The fifth reference is, of course, the article by Dr Máire de Paor, already referred to, in the 'Seanchas Ardmhacha' of 1961.

The sixth and final reference is to be found in *Down Survey 2000*, in an article by Cormac Bourke, entitled 'What the Pilgrim Saw';

> Less easily attributed to a specific centre is the post-medieval, perhaps seventeenth-century, shrine of St Patrick's jaw (St Malachy's College, Belfast), which manifests the last gasp of medieval enshrining practice.

The Savage family of Dunturk, between Castlewellan and The Spa, held the shrine in the nineteenth century and a County Down connection is not in doubt.

The golden age of ecclesiastical insignia is now past, although ceremony still has its place on occasion. But we do well to recognise the values of the middle ages, if only to put our own values in perspective. The metalwork considered here was made with posterity in mind, because the saints would be saints always. As we contemplate Christian treasures on exhibition, though we might feel ever so detached, we are but part of an endless chain of viewers.

And yet the relic did not feature in the Down and Connor Diocesan celebrations for the Patrician year of 1961!

Canon Noel Conway a past President of Saint Malachy's, has informed the author that the relic was kept in an archive case, these were loaned to the Ulster Museum in the 1990s and displayed there along with the Shrine of Saint Patrick's Hand.

The portion of the relic supposedly enclosed in the altar of Saint Patrick's, Derriaghy, has long since been lost. We know that by 1854 the jaw-bone, as recounted in the *Ulster Journal of Archaeology*, still retained a double tooth, now missing. Máire De Paor tells us that the Cullen family still had possession of the shrine and jaw-bone in 1854. O'Laverty tells us that Bishop Dorrian purchased the shrine and relic from the Cullen family of Derriaghy. It seems likely then that after 1854 the shrine and relic were placed in the care of St Malachy's College, Belfast, and apart from the six references in between, the shrine and relic only emerge back into the light of day as recently as 2006!

Feargal Patrick McGrady
*The Background and History of the Relic and Shrine of the
Jaw-bone of Saint Patrick*, 2010

The Bell of Saint Patrick

This Bell of St. Patrick, which, we understand, is to be carried in the June Eucharistic Congress Procession has a most interesting history. In a MS. of Irish poems preserved in the Bodleian Lib. of Oxford, there is a poem attributed to St. Colmcille and purporting to be addressed to the bell. I shall quote a translation of the first three stanzas:

My love to thee, O smooth and melodius bell,
Which wast on the Tailgenn's breast,
Which was permitted me by Christ without guile,
The raising, the delivering of it.

Ten years and three just score,
Was this bell with all its graces
On the breast of Patrick, first apostle,
And he withered not beneath the stone.

I command, for the safe keeping of my bell,
Eight who shall be noble, illustrious,
A priest and a deacon among them,
That my bell may not deteriorate.

The A.U. 1044 record a predatory expedition by Niall, King of Ailech against U. Meith and against Cuailgne in which he carried off 1200 cows and a multitude of captives in revenge for the violation of the Bell of the Will. At this period the bell, by orders of the Archbishop of Armagh and the King of Ireland, was enshrined in gold and silver and arrangements made for its safe keeping. The name of its maor or keeper was O'Maelchallan and in 1441 we find it recorded that Patrick O'Mulchallynd, a keeper of this bell, held lands in Ballyclog (townland of the Bell), near Stewartstown, Co. Tyrone. The bell remained in the possession

of the Mulholland and O'Mellan families (near relations) for generations, and in 1758 Bernard Mulholland of Maghera, Co. Derry, still held the precious relic. His grandson, Henry Mulholland, having been educated for the priesthood, became later a school-teacher in Edenduffcarrick, between Antrim and Randalstown, and having no surviving relatives, handed over the bell and shrine and a copy of an Irish Bible to his former pupil and lifelong friend, Mr Adam M'Clean of Belfast. In 1819 the latter preserved the bell. Dr. Todd, of Trinity College, received a donation of it from Mr M'Clean on his death-bed, and the National Museum of Dublin purchased it from Dr. Todd. After a chequered history and many adventures, St. Patrick's bell now rests in the Museum of the National Library of Dublin.

Anon.
Down and Connor's Historical Society's Journal, 1931

Shrine of St Patrick's Bell

This shrine was made about the eleventh century as a container for the bell. Its side panels and crests are decorated in the so-called 'urnes' style in which large beasts are interlaced with thin ribbon-like snakes. An inscription on the margins of the back plate tells us that it was made by Condulig Ua hInmainen and his sons for Domhnall Ua Lochlainn

(King of Ireland, 1094–1121). Domhnall Mac Amhalgadha was then bishop of Armagh, and Cathalan Ua Maelchallain was the 'keeper of the bell', a position his family was to retain until the end of the eighteenth century.

Patrick F. Wallace
A Guide to the National Museum of Ireland, 2000

The Shrine of St. Patrick's Bell

Adam McClean was something of an antiquarian, and how he came into possession of that priceless and very exquisite specimen of ancient Irish art, 'the shrine of St. Patrick's bell', is an interesting story.

An inscription on the shrine shows that it was made at the expense of Donal MacLoughlin, king of Ireland, for Donal MacAmalagaid, primate of Armagh, at the close of the eleventh century. The name of the hereditary keeper of the bell is also inscribed on the cover, and it is remarkable that it was in the possession of one family, the O'Mulhollans, from the period in which the shrine was made until it passed into Adam McClean's hands. The names of the artists who made the shrine are also given in the inscription, and from the expensive materials, so profusely lavished on it, it is manifest that the bell itself, the principal object of veneration, had been viewed as a precious relic of antiquity so long ago as the eleventh century. This was apparent from at least one circumstance. The shrine was firmly closed around the bell, the piety of its possessors doubtless esteeming it, from a feeling of veneration for the memory of the saint to whom it once had belonged, too sacred for exposure to the touch or even sight of ordinary persons.

For generations the shrine and the bell were in the custody of the O'Mulhollan family, and they were bequeathed to Adam McClean by its last survivor. The name of Mulhollan, which in the original Gaelic is Maol-Choluim, signifies the servant of Saint Colm Cille (of Doire). And it is a remarkable fact that although for many years he was in destitute circumstances the thought of selling the priceless treasure never once entered the custodian's mind; on the contrary, to ensure its safety, he was in the habit of burying it in a strong oaken box and removing it when he changed his place of abode. He died at the little village of Eden-duff-carrick, which formerly existed within the grounds of Shane's castle in Antrim, and once on a day I made pilgrimage to the spot where he is buried.

On the shore of Lough Neagh I found it, among spreading woods whose trees were giants when Shane O'Neill himself was but a dark, slender lad. Beside the ruined walls and great underground vaults of a castle, the little graveyard was a green space apart, where, at my lightest footfall amongst the moss-grown graveslabs, a startled blackbird left across the green silence a trail of golden laughter, his swift shadow falling where the ground-ivy spread around the stones a soft carpet of mauve and green under the branchy trees.

Of the village of Eden-duff-carrick there was no trace – the graveyard told its story – but a certain Henry Mulhollan of this place was the last hereditary keeper of the shrine of Saint Patrick's bell, the bell of the will. And the story runs that he had studied for the priesthood, but for some reason became schoolmaster in the village school instead. When master Mulhollan became old, and when he was on his deathbed, of one of his former pupils who had been kind to him in his declining years and who was present, he made this request – that he would go out and dig under a tree in a certain part of the garden, and there, the old man said, he would find an oaken chest, which, he stated, contained all that he valued most on earth, and which he now wished to bestow on his good friend and former pupil, Adam McClean.

The chest on being discovered was found to contain a bible printed in the Gaelic language, and Saint Patrick's bell with its marvellously beautiful and world-famous shrine. These unique and matchless treasures were kept by Adam McClean in his house at No. 4 Donegall square south for many years, and after his death were sold by his sons to Dr. Todd, of Trinity College, Dublin, for £50, and Dr. Todd's executors, in turn, sold them to the custodians of the Royal Irish Academy for the sum of £500.

And so, it is gratifying to be able to chronicle that, after all the huxtering, the priceless shrine and the bell of Saint Patrick found at last their true resting place, a niche in the treasure house of Dublin, the capital of Catholic Ireland. And that is the story told of the discovery, by Adam McClean, of Belfast, at the little village of Eden-duff-carrick (Eadan dubh carraig), near Randalstown, in the county of Antrim, of the oaken treasure chest containing Saint Patrick's bell and its shrine, about the year 1819.

Cathal O'Byrne
As I Roved Out: A Book of the North, 1946

St. Patrick In Art

Curiously enough early representations of St. Patrick are extremely rare in Ireland, perhaps because their beloved saint was sufficiently enshrined in the hearts of the Irish people, but more probably because of the destruction of monuments by their two enemies – time and man. No pre-Norman effigy or sculpture exists, and even later figures are rare.

A little figure, beautifully modelled in silver, adorning the O'Dea crozier, that lovely treasure of the Limerick diocese, is perhaps the earliest, dating from the year 1418. The saint is shown with two staves in his hands with which he spurns the dragon-like reptile beneath his feet.

An interesting stone slab in the National Museum, Dublin

shows the saint with his traditional snake, in a curious flat incised style of carving.

On a tomb in St. Canice's Cathedral, Kilkenny, of about 1500, the saint is shown between an unusual representation of Christus Regnans and a sainted king.

Coming to our own times, there is Boris Anrep's fine mosaic in Mullingar, which combines a traditional pre-christian Mediterranean technique, mosaic, with a vigorous modern treatment: Saint Patrick, as our Patron and a holy man of an audacious and vigorous mind and personality merits the best that our modern artists can create. May he inspire them to produce worthy and lovely statues for our churches.

John Hunt
The Furrow, 1953

The Iconography of St. Patrick

It is safe to say that if St. Patrick revisited at the present time this 'Island of Saints', and made a circuit of our churches, he would not know himself, or be able to identify himself (except by an inscription) from the other saints and holy personages therein represented.

This seems strange in a country which prides itself on having clung so tenaciously to the faith he brought us, despite unparalleled persecution and proscription.

That we should have no exact portrait of his face and features is not to be wondered at, as no contemporary representation of him has come down to us, but that we should disguise him so completely that neither he himself nor any of his contemporaries could to-day identify him was hardly to be expected. The modern tall figure with long sweeping beard, the Gothic mitre, the richly embroidered vestments, and the elaborately designed metal-headed crozier, would all seem to him as something new and strange. But nothing perhaps would amuse him more than to see this figure representing himself as treading on a nest of serpents, when he called to mind the thirty odd years he had spent in Ireland during which he had never seen a serpent ...

Let me now introduce a man called Thomas Messingham. Unfortunately very little is known about him, beyond that he was a native of Meath, was educated in Paris, was ordained there as a secular priest, and in time became Superior of the Irish College there. His name occurs in the correspondence of the period from 1614 till 1630, after which it ceases. During this time he was a very active worker. When he died is not known. His birth, in the diocese of Meath, was probably between 1570 and 1580. Born at a time he, as a boy, saw no images in the churches; and illustrated books in the homes of even well-to-do people were then almost non-existent. He went to France in his teens as a student, and the chances are a thousand-to-one that he never saw in Ireland a traditional representation of St. Patrick

His written works deal with Irish ecclesiastical history, and among these is 'Florilegium Insulae Sanctorum', a folio volume, published in Paris in 1624. As a frontispiece to this work appears representations of SS. Patrick, Brigid and Colmcille.

His artist or engraver was 'L. Gaultier, Paris', and the plate has the further inscription 'T. Messingham fecit, 1624'. Whether Messingham drew the figures himself or not is immaterial: the ideas they represent are his.

This frontispiece is the beginning and prototype of all those countless thousands of bearded and mitred figures of St. Patrick which have since appeared.

This is the origin of the pseudo 'tradition' – originating in Paris, with a French engraver and an Irish priest of English or Pale extraction, who was born after practically all the traditionally Irish representations of our saint had been destroyed, and who spent all his adult life outside his native land. This portrait of St. Patrick was copied into other works, notably the 1809 Dublin edition of Jocelin's Life of St. Patrick. But such works were known to only a limited number of learned men, and would hardly suffice to make the mitred 'St Patrick' a popular conception. This latter was accomplished by the issue in 1789, and some subsequent years, of what was known as 'Cronebane Tokens', namely halfpenny copper coins, made of copper from the Cronebane mine in Co. Wicklow to the east of the river Avoca. The obverse bears the bust of a bearded St. Patrick with a mitre and pastoral staff. The design was made by Hancock of Birmingham. Copper coins were then scarce in Ireland, and these coins circulated everywhere in this country among rich and poor alike. It was the first time in two hundred years that the average Irishman had seen a figure of St. Patrick, and it became fixed in the popular imagination, and so remains to this day. 'Sure only for the beard we would not know him,' said a pious old woman to me, referring to a picture of our patron saint. Our Catholic churches began to be reopened and rebuilt about the same time as the Cronebane coins appeared, and the bearded, mitred figure of the saint became the vogue in the churches, and can now be counted by the thousand in stone, stained glass, painting, and engraving. Such is the modern pseudo 'tradition', its origin, and development.

What then, it must be asked, was the genuine native tradition before the middle of the 16th Century? ... The chief representations of our saint that have survived are in carvings on stone, and some of these are on monuments that have been exposed to the weather and to the destructive instincts of human nature for a thousand years, so that they are now much worn and indistinct. In addition to these we have a few figures stamped or cast in metal and now also much worn and fairly indistinct. Even these all fall short by centuries of St. Patrick's era, and for this last gap we have to fall back on other evidence.

Let us first take the saint's face. When in 1930 I claimed that he was beardless I stood almost alone. The theory was too novel, too staggering for most people to accept. A learned friend in Dublin wrote me – 'I have read your article: you'll want a much better razor before you succeed in shaving St. Patrick.' However, in the very next year –1931– unexpected assistance came along, and my friend now admits that St. Patrick is as clean-shaven as any young Maynooth priest. The assistance I refer to was the publication of that great but, as yet, little known work 'The Crosses and Culture of Ireland', by Doctor Kingsley Porter, Professor of Fine Arts in Harvard University, U.S.A., who so tragically met his death in a storm off the coast of Co. Donegal two years later. This distinguished man took up the examination of our Irish High Crosses, and brought to this study an immense fund of learning and a breadth of view that was anything but insular.

On page 21 of this book – 'The Crosses and Culture of Ireland' – he says 'No example of the representative arts of the time of Patrick has come down to us. The iconography of the saint was no doubt formed at a later period, and on the basis of posthumous legends.' Then he remarks on the paucity of representations of Patrick on the High Crosses, and continues – 'Indeed it has been generally supposed that Patrick does not appear at all in the early iconography of Ireland. That is an exaggeration, for certain hitherto unexplained panels of the cross (of King Flann of Clonmacnoise) without doubt represent scenes of his life. The upper panel on the south side of the shaft of this cross has never been explained. In it we see standing an ecclesiastic, certainly a bishop or an abbot, because of the tau crozier or bachall which he holds. The head of the saint is much damaged, but the face seems beardless. Above him hovers an angel. There can, I think, be little doubt that the sculptor intended it to represent St. Patrick with his familiar angel Victor, who is constantly referred to in "The Tripartite Life". As the most ancient portrait of St. Patrick this relief is of no common interest But it is not only on this panel of the cross that the apostle appears. The relief shows us St. Patrick designated as pilgrim, by the wallet hung round his neck, carrying his tau crozier, receiving the monastic tonsure at the hands of St. Martin. It is to be remarked that in the relief both saints are beardless – shaving the beard was as much part of the Irish tonsure as shaving the head.'

Another panel of the Clonmacnoise is interpreted by Dr. Porter as a representation of the saint banishing the demons from the 'Rock', and he remarks – 'The face is clearly beardless.'

Henry Morris
Down and Connor Historical Society's Journal, 1936

The Cross of Saints Patrick and Columba

Standing close to, and at mid-morning literally in the shadow of, the Round Tower of the old Columban monastery, is the Cross of Saints Patrick and Columba, 3.30 m high, which gets its name from an inscription proclaiming that this is the cross of Saints Patrick and Columba. This inscription which, unusually for the Irish crosses, is in Latin, may well document the involvement in the erection of the cross of Máel Brigte mac Tornáin who, after 891 was abbot both of Armagh (founded by St. Patrick) and of Kells, a Columban foundation, providing us with a probable late-ninth-century date for the cross. The panels of this cross seem less disciplined yet demonstrate a greater freedom in design by not having its biblical panels formally separated by frames, instead of which they are either kept apart by interlace or are simply juxtaposed above or beside one another …

North side
The identity of the figure on the end of the arm is uncertain. So, too, is that of the two figures on top of the shaft, but as the one seen on the right may hold up a panel bearing a ringed cross, we may have here a representation of the two saints mentioned in the inscription. If so, these would be the earliest surviving representations of either of these two churchmen.

Peter Harbison
Irish High Crosses, 1994

Tiepolo's St Patrick Altarpiece

Tiepolo scholars have dismissed St. Patrick as the protagonist of an altarpiece by that painter at Padua. Here, Dr. Catherine Whistler who recently completed her doctoral thesis at University College Dublin on the late religious paintings of Giambattista Tiepolo, re-examines the question and argues for the reinstatement of St. Patrick.

Much confusion has reigned over the title, subject-matter and provenance of a sparkling, richly-executed altarpiece of c.1746 by Giambattista Tiepolo, now in the Museo Civico, Padua.

'San Patrizio vescovo d'Irlanda', Giambattista Tiepolo, 1746

The painting is displayed there under the title of *St. Paulinus of Aquileia* bearing witness to the influence of scholarly opinion which has lately rejected the traditional identification of the saint as St. Patrick, Bishop of Ireland. On the evidence of the altarpiece's appearance alone a number of possible candidates could be proposed for the principal role of the bishop-saint, who bears no unique attributes. But a closer look shows that two distinct activities are being commemorated in this painting.

The venerable saint, pulling his stiff, heavy vestments to him, addresses himself to the humble, reverent figures of a country woman, her hair tied up in a kerchief, and to her young son at his feet. Their solemn attention to the saint's words is mirrored in the still absorption of the exotic bearded spectator who faces them across the painting. By contrast to this silent concentration, a totally different kind of attention is registered by the tense, eager group on the right who strain forward in astonishment and awe, transfixed by the saint's miracle-making gesture. Their emotion is released by the excitement of the figures high up on the loggia behind, while the saint's impressive stance finds its corollary in the rapid flight, legs kicking, of the demon which disappears off in the upper left of the painting. The bishop-saint is therefore to be reverenced for his preaching and his powers against evil spirits. The subject of the exorcism would appear to be the rather dishevelled dark-haired woman, stilled now into wonderment. But the real theme of the altarpiece is the impact of the saint's supernatural powers and hypnotic presence on a rapt group of individuals, ranging from the miserably clad, crippled old man clutching his rosary beads, to the opulent blonde woman in a lace ruff and pearls, a group with whom the spectator is invited to identify. The setting of the altarpiece is a symbolic one, typical of Tiepolo's mature religious works, where Veronesian precedents allow for the use of Sansovino's architecture to create a lofty, noble zone appropriate to miracles or sacred gatherings. Yet this rich setting intermingles with the world of common humanity, for the pedestal supporting the saint is cracked and it stands upon a worn brick pavement, while the old man's crutch and straw basket jut forward into the space of the church itself, inviting the participation of a wider audience.

That Tiepolo was given a free hand with the subject seems clear from a number of pen and ink studies for the composition. In these drawings, which apart from anything else demonstrate the care he was willing to bestow upon a religious commission for a monastery church when more prestigious works were demanding his attention in this busy decade, Giambattista experimented with the arrangement of the human figures. In some he gave prominence to the young boy, in others to the old man, or to a seated woman, but ultimately granted all of them equal weight in the final version, where each individual becomes in his own fashion caught up in the saint's charisma. For this reason the painting has been interpreted in different ways as depicting the saint healing a sick man, or preaching a sermon, or exorcizing a possessed boy.

The altarpiece was executed for the Lateran Canons of San Giovanni di Verdara in Padua, and not for the Jesuit church there as is sometimes stated. Early guide books describe the painting as the *Miracle of St. Patrick*, standing in the first chapel on the left in San Giovanni di Verdara. However, Domenico Tiepolo identified the altarpiece as *St. Paulinus of Aquileia* in the catalogue he compiled of etchings by his father and etchings after his father's paintings in 1775. Domenico was dealing with a large body of work five years after Giambattista's death, moreover he is not the most reliable of compilers since he gave the more recent *St. Paschal Baylon*, executed in 1767–69, the title of S. Diego, although Giambattista had never executed a painting of that saint. Art historians have lately followed Domenico's identification, preferring to see the local saint, Patriarch of Aquileia, as a more likely subject for an altarpiece in the Veneto than that of the remote figure of St. Patrick.

However, St. Paulinus was a rather obscure ninth-century saint who had his patriarchal seat at Cividale, in Friuli, far from Venice's influence, and was renowned, if anything, for his political importance as negotiator between Charlemagne and the Byzantine Empire, rather than for the miracles or cult followings; indeed representations of this saint are rare. Although the saint's pastoral writings were newly published in Latin for a clerical audience in Venice in 1737, studies of patron saints and cults of saints in the Veneto do not record any trace of popular devotion to St. Paulinus. On the other hand, since a relic of St. Patrick was preserved at Piazza Vecchia, midway between Padua and Venice, Patrick enjoyed something of a cult-following locally. In Venice, St. Patrick's feastday was celebrated with special devotions at the church of the Carita by the Lateran Canons there. The real clue to the correct identity of the saint in Tiepolo's altarpiece lies in the devotional traditions of the Order who commissioned the painting. The Lateran Canons, famed in Padua for their erudition and piety, regarded St. Patrick as one of their own. A life of St. Patrick written by a Lateran Canon at Bologna in 1657, records how the saint visited Rome after his Irish captivity, and how at the church of St. John Lateran he was received into the Order of the Lateran Canons by Pope Celestine, who then blessed his future mission to Ireland. The Canons Regular of St. Augustine, of whom the congregation of the Lateran formed a part, were enthusiastic promoters of the cult of St. Patrick all over Europe. The saint was listed in the calendar of saints of their Order; the Office of St. Patrick was included in their breviary. By the eighteenth century a special litany celebrated St. Patrick as a preacher, as a formidable power against evil spirits and as one of the glories of the Order of the Canons Regular of St. Augustine. Tiepolo's altarpiece commemorates these very qualities in the bishop-saint who can now be re-instated in his former glory as St. Patrick.

In the eighteenth century the cult of St. Patrick was

widespread in Europe, whether because hagiography or strong local traditions had associated certain places with the life of the saint, or because devotion originally introduced by Irish missionaries and pilgrims had been sustained and elaborated over the centuries, or because of the interest of particular religious orders in promoting the cult. For example, from the evidence of early sources St. Patrick is believed to have studied at Auxerre, while according to tradition he visited the monastery founded by St. Martin at Marmoutier, near Tours. Relics inspire devotion and stimulate belief: in France relics of St. Patrick found their way to Peronne in the seventh century, and to the cathedral at Sens by the twelfth century, while in Italy relics were kept, amongst other places, at Torre S. Patrizio in the diocese of Fermo, and at the church of S. Maria di Loreto in Rome. Thanks to the fervour of Irish pilgrims, St. Patrick was long venerated in the German province of Baden-Wurttemberg, where local devotion eventually enshrined the saint as a patron of agriculture; in the province of Styria, in Austria, St. Patrick enjoyed a similar role as protector of cattle. Pilgrimage routes over the Alps to Rome were also dotted with centres of devotion to St. Patrick, such as Vertova, near Bergamo, and the town of S. Patrizio near Conselice in the province of Ravenna. Irish colleges and seminaries in Italy and Spain, and religious orders also helped to promote the cult of St. Patrick in Europe. Thus the Franciscan order celebrated the feast of the saint from the late fourteenth century, the Benedictines encouraged devotion in many centres including Torre S. Patrizio, as did the Augustinians who held that the saint had lived according to the Rule of St. Augustine. Examples of Augustinian interest in the saint include the chapel dedicated to him at Pollauberg in Styria, an important spot on medieval pilgrimage routes, and the altar and altarpiece to the saint in the church of the Lateran Canons in Bologna, S. Giovanni in Monte.

An unbroken series of celebratory biographies in the sixteenth and seventeenth centuries confirms the strength of literary and religious interest in the saint and his works. However, no internationally accepted unique image of the saint emerged in this period as an iconographic type, despite widespread devotion. Thus it was easy for Domenico Tiepolo to misinterpret his father's representation of the saint. Ireland's turbulent religious history prevented the production of exemplary images of the patron saint, while many centres of Patrician devotion in Europe had lost their medieval importance as meeting-points on pilgrimage routes, or as centres of learning, and images of the saint scattered in the development of a distinctive iconography.

Early Irish representations show a clean-shaven bishop-saint with a crozier which is sometimes in the shape of a curved staff, or more often a staff topped with a slim cross with arms of equal length above a horizontal bar. This type seems to have found its way to southern Germany, for some early eighteenth century statues of the saint in Baden-Wurttemberg show a beardless bishop-saint with farm animals at his feet, and interestingly the shamrock is included either together with the saint's book, or as a decorative motif. The shamrock does not appear elsewhere in Europe as an attribute of the saint, so perhaps here it was somehow an Irish importation. Irish tradition had long associated the shamrock with St. Patrick's missionary activities, and it was a clearly recognizable national emblem by the reign of Henry IV when it was used in the coinage of the realm. Patriotism and devotion could be fused in an instrument of political propaganda as when Confederate Catholics in Kilkenny, in 1642, issued coins from a mint set up by the Papal Nuncio showing St. Patrick holding the shamrock before an assembly of people. In Europe, given the lack of Irish religious images and probably ignorance of popular Irish legend, written sources generally provided material for artistic representation. The tale of St. Patrick's use of the shamrock to illustrate, in a sermon at Tara, the concept of the Trinity, is not mentioned in any of the early lives of the saint.

A sixteenth-century narrative cycle in stained glass in the church of S. Patrice at Rouen in France illustrates miracles and scenes from the life of the saint, many of them apocryphal, but does not include the shamrock legend. Instead, in Europe, the saint is strongly identified with the vanquishing of evil spirits. Giuseppe Mitelli (1634–1718) in his frontispiece for the Lateran Canon Giacomo Certani's *Il Mosè dell'Ibernia*, published in Bologna in 1686, includes as objects associated with St. Patrick a crozier, a book, a bishop's mitre and a bell. Mitelli, an expert book illustrator whose father Agostino had been court artist to Philip IV of Spain, designed a dramatic but essentially elegant scene where St. Patrick banishes demons as he kneels in the open air before a crucifix. The white-bearded energetic saint flings his bell at three large devils who writhe and struggle gracefully in their flight, anxious to escape the holy wrath of this commanding figure. A seventeenth-century altarpiece in the church of St. Bavo in Brussels shows the saint again in the company of demons: he stands victorious in full bishop's regalia as a cherub spears a demon at his feet. Even in a native Irish painting by James Barry, the *Baptism of the King of Cashel*, of 1760–63, the saint is not given any distinctive emblems or attributes other than bishop's robes, mitre and crozier, a long white beard, and a venerable appearance. However, attributes might have seemed superfluous in this unmistakeably Patrician subject.

It seems as though the image of St. Patrick proposed by the Irish priest Thomas Messingham in his *Florilegium Insulae Sanctorum* published in Paris in 1624 became a prototype for future representations in Europe, superseding the early native iconography of a clean-shaven saint, placing him in contemporary liturgical vestments instead of seeking historical accuracy, and ignoring any popular associations of the saint with the shamrock. The design of Tiepolo's altarpiece seems to bear some resemblance to Messingham's depiction of St. Patrick. The Lateran Canons at Padua with their distinguished library and their veneration of the saint could well have brought this image to Tiepolo's attention. It too concentrates on the saint's vanquishing of evil spirits, the power of his words, and the reverence of the human audience. However, its flatness of delivery and its old-fashioned hieratic structure are transformed beyond all recognition in the subtlety and vitality of Tiepolo's altarpiece. This painting stands as a colourful testimony to the strength of a singular devotional tradition, and as a striking example of Tiepolo's fresh approach to religious themes where picturesque and decorative elements are firmly anchored by clarity, realism and a concern with the human spectator.

Dr Catherine Whistler
Irish Arts Review, 1985

An illustration of St Patrick taken from Thomas Messingham, *Florilegium Insulae Sanctorum*, Paris 1624.

A Mosaic of St. Patrick

When Christianity emerged from the catacombs, what Walter Pater calls 'the aesthetic charm of the Catholic Church, her evocative power over all that is eloquent in the better mind of man, her outward comeliness …' began to be lavished on the beautifying of her places of worship. Attracted by the exquisite beauty of mosaic materials (marble, enamel, precious stones, gold, silver, mother-of-pearl) the early Christians adopted it to cover and decorate the interior walls of their churches which were usually built of brick, and the art of mosaic flourished until fresco, oil, and tempera painting came into fashion with the Renaissance. But it was not its mere material beauty that captivated the artists of the time; they found mosaic material eminently suitable for translating spiritual subjects into visions of mystic significance and into forms stripped of earthly sensuousness.

A radical change came with the Renaissance. Mural decoration became pictorial, and gestures and expressions grew complicated, elaborate and naturalistic. The luscious beauty of Renaissance painters lured mosaic into imitating effects of their fluid media, forcing them to perform acrobatic feats to emulate effects alien to the nature of hard materials. The original, simple expressiveness was lost, and gradually mosaic was reduced to a secondary place as a commercial craft.

Many modern mosaics executed by commercial firms imitate too closely the coloured drawings set out by artists who have little contact with the material of mosaic itself, who are ignorant of, or disregard, its limitations, and who do not reveal the peculiar character of the material. Divorced from the personality of the artist such mosaics can only become 'petrified' coloured drawings, deprived of all vitality.

In recent years there has been a revival of interest in the true nature of mosaic, and one of the outstanding personalities in its re-discovery is Boris Anrep, the only example of whose work in Ireland was recently executed at Mullingar Cathedral.

The son of a Russian statesman and scientist, Boris Anrep was born in Russia in 1888. He graduated from the Imperial School of Law and was attached to St. Petersburg University; but Art attracted him from early days, and abandoning his academic pursuits, he went to Paris to study painting. After several years of study he became keenly interested in the Early Christian and Byzantine Arts, in which he has since specialized. Mosaic became his particular subject and he travelled to Italy, Greece and the Middle East in search of the best examples of this art. He also worked in several factories to discover the defects in modern methods of mosaic production; the revival of true mosaic art became his ambition.

After the Russian Revolution in 1917 Anrep settled in England, where his chief works can be found, the more important being at the Tate and the National Galleries, London, the Bank of England, the Greek Cathedral, Bayswater, London, the Kier Chapel near Sterling, Birmingham Museum and Westminister Cathedral, where he executed a mosaic of Blessed Oliver Plunket. He now lives in Paris.

Shortly before his translation to Armagh in 1946, Dr. D'Alton, then Bishop of Meath, commissioned Anrep to decorate the chapel of St. Patrick in the Cathedral of Christ the King, Mullingar; but it was not until the summer of 1948 that the work was completed. The design represents St. Patrick lighting the fire at Slane.

The centre of the picture is occupied by the large figure of St. Patrick and the scale of the figure is calculated in relation to the surrounding architectural features, with a view to making it a dominant subject. The Saint raises in his right hand a Cross, in the other he holds a lighted torch. The flames rise from burning logs and branches arranged in the form of a Christogram. Behind him is a group of followers with the two princesses who had embraced the Faith. A paschal lamb is in the arms of one of the group; another holds a mitre, the symbol of Patrick's episcopal dignity. The treatment of St. Patrick's figure and face, the vigour of his movement, the bare head, the flowing vestments are splendidly suggestive of his Apostolic mission.

'St Patrick lighting the fire at Slane', Boris Anrep, 1948

In the right-hand corner stands an idol which has been reproduced from an authentic Celtic model. The idol is disintegrated by lightning from Heaven at the impact of St. Patrick's Faith in the triumph of Christ over Irish paganism. Snakes crawl away from underneath the rocks upon which the idol stands.

The upper part of the composition is occupied by the representation of Christ Enthroned, flanked by two Angels. Our Lord holds a pastoral staff as a reminder of the legendary Bacall Iosa. Christ's feet rest on the globe of the sun which shines over the Saint's progress.

The lower portion of the mosaic is occupied by a Latin translation of St. Patrick's 'Breast-Plate'. This with decorative panels forms a base for the picture. Of these decorative panels the central one, immediately behind the altar table, represents a decorative motif from the Castledermot high cross. At the base of that cross is a strange figure representing a bound man with a cock's head, and it has been interpreted as the shrouded figure of the devil placed in a tomb with knees pressed to his chin, the normal position for early burial. It is assumed that the reason for placing such a motif at the foot of the high cross is to signify the victory of the Cross over the power of Hell. Anrep has adopted it for the same reason.

The colour-scheme of the mosaic has been chosen with a view to impart light and transparency which, in the opinion of the artist, is essential for the style, the subject of the mosaic and its place in the Cathedral. In sympathy with the general atmosphere of the architecture it enhances the spiritual quality of mosaic treatment. The lightness of the general tone is relieved in places by bolder colour to allow the eye to follow the rhythm of the composition.

John Brady
The Furrow, 1950

St. Patrick's Coin

It was while the king [Charles I] was an exile from London, without a treasury or a mint, and while his Irish army, unpaid and neglected, were often in want of the common necessities of life, that a call was made – July 8th, 1643 – upon the Irish loyalists during the military leadership of the marquis, afterwards duke, of Ormonde in this country, to send in their plate to be melted down and coined for the royal use. This call was responded to by plate being sent in to about the value of £1200; but the king, on the 20th May following, ordered money to be regularly minted, with "C.R." and a crown in one side, and the value on the other ...

The next series of coins to which I call your attention are those peculiarly identified with Kilkenny, and known under the names of 'St. Patrick's coin', 'Rebel coin', and 'Confederate coin', and are presumed to have been struck under the Confederate coincil of Kilkenny in 1642 or 1643 ...

Simon's [James Simon, author of *An Essay on Irish Coins*, 1810] description of these coins is as follows: 'These Half-pennies have on one side the figure of a king crowned, with a radiant crown, kneeling and playing on the harp, and over the harp the imperial crown of England of a different metal from that of the coin, that is brass upon copper, or copper upon brass, with this inscription, FLOREAT REX. Reverse, the figure of St. Patrick mitred, and standing with a crosier in his right hand, and a leaf of trefoil in his left [Simon confounds the terms right for left and left for right], which he holds out to the people about him, and on his left side the arms of the city of Dublin, three castles, with this

legend ECCE GREX. The farthing has likewise on one side a king crowned and playing on a harp, a crown of copper or brass over it and round, FLOREAT REX. Reverse, St. Patrick mitred, holding in his left hand a double or metropolitan cross, a church behind him, and stretching out his right hand  over a parcel of serpents and other venomous creatures as if driving them out of the church, and alluding to the protestants, called in the before-mentioned act the puritanical, – the malignant party; inscription, QVIESCAT PLEBS.' Simon here alludes to the act of the Confederate assembly of Kilkenny.

Robert Cane
Transactions of the Kilkenny Archaeological Society, 1851

5

MYTH AND LEGEND

The myths, legends and traditions surrounding St Patrick are legion. In early hagiography he was represented as a wonder worker who could, amongst other wonders, make fire from ice, change himself and his followers into deer, raise druids bodily into the air and drop them to their death, restore an old man to youth, dispel darkness, raise people (indeed, once a horse, and once a giant) from the dead and drink poison to no ill effect. In various eras in the history of Irish Christianity these stories were not only believed, but their proponent was revered for his prowess – a prowess that was self-evidently God-given. In this, there is a continuity with early and medieval biblical scholars, who argued that the two-fold purpose of the miracles of Jesus Christ (and by extension of St Patrick) was to demonstrate his divine powers, and to confirm the authenticity of his religious revelation. Not until the Reformation did religious communities seriously question the reality of miracles in people's everyday lives.

The Patrician legends of the snakes and the shamrock are so intimately associated with the saint that they cannot now be disassociated from his story. The shamrock was first mentioned in connection with the mission of St Patrick by Threlkeld in his work of natural history – *Synopsis Stirpium Hibernarum*, published in 1727. The idea of teaching the very difficult doctrine of the Trinity through the physical medium of the tri-foil shamrock is so appropriate that listeners can immediately understand (or believe that they understand) and become believers. Likewise, the Irish and all the world are more prepared than not to believe that the first use of the shamrock in this way was indeed by St Patrick.

Likewise the legend that Patrick banished the snakes from Ireland. The fact that Ireland has been snake-free forever does not diminish the power of the legend. In historical religious metaphor, snakes and reptiles were commonly used to denote evil or the devil. The now common image of Patrick standing on a rock with snakes writhing underfoot is proof positive of the life and longevity of this iconic legend. And, as a consequence of the reality and legend of the life of St Patrick, the spread of the cult of St Patrick – the man and the legend – has continued from the fifth into the twenty-first century.

In a previous chapter we see the spread of devotion to Patrick on the Continent of Europe, in France, Spain, Italy and Germany. The same devotion travelled westward, also; carried in the hearts of expatriate Irish men and women who founded churches and societies dedicated to St Patrick, the patron saint of Ireland. Despite scholarly disagreement concerning facts and aspects of his life, it seems totally appropriate to suggest, as did William Philbin in the first extract in this anthology:

'There is no greater name in Irish history than Patrick son of Calpruinn ...'

St. Patrick Was a Gentleman

Oh! St. Patrick was a gentleman,
Who came of decent people;
He built a church in Dublin town,
And on it put a steeple.
His father was a Gallagher;
His mother was a Brady;
His aunt was an O'Shaughnessy,
His uncle an O'Grady.
So, success attend St. Patrick's fist,
For he's a saint so clever;
O! he gave the snakes and toads a twist,
And bothered them forever!

The Wicklow hills are very high,
And so's the Hill of Howth, sir;
But there's a hill, much bigger still,
Much higher nor them both, sir.
'Twas on the top of this high hill
St Patrick preached his sarmint
That drove the frogs into the bogs,
And banished all the varmint.
So, success attend St. Patrick's fist,
For he's a saint so clever;
O! he gave the snakes and toads a twist,
And bothered them forever!

There's not a mile in Ireland's isle
Where dirty varmin musters,
But there he put his dear fore-foot,
And murdered them in clusters.
The toads went pop, the frogs went hop,

Slap-dash into the water;
And the snakes committed suicide
To save themselves from slaughter.
So, success attend St. Patrick's fist,
For he's a saint so clever;
O! he gave the snakes and toads a twist,
And bothered them forever!

Nine hundred thousand reptiles blue
He charmed them with sweet discourses,
And dined on them at Killaloe
In soups and second courses.
Where blind worms crawling in the grass
Disgusted all the nation,
He gave them a rise, which opened their eyes
To a sense of their situation.
So, success attend St. Patrick's fist,
For he's a saint so clever;
O! he gave the snakes and toads a twist,
And bothered them forever!

No wonder that those Irish lads
Should be so gay and frisky,
For sure St. Pat he taught them that,
As well as making whiskey;
No wonder that the saint himself
Should understand distilling,
Since his mother kept a shebeen shop
In the town of Enniskillen.
So, success attend St. Patrick's fist,
For he's a saint so clever;
O! he gave the snakes and toads a twist,
And bothered them forever!

O! was I but fortunate
As to be back in Munster,
'Tis I'd be bound that from that ground
I never more would once stir.
For there St. Patrick planted turf,
And plenty of the praties,
With pigs galore, ma gra, ma 'store,
And cabbages—and ladies!
Then my blessing on St. Patrick's fist,
For he's the darling saint O!
O! he gave the snakes and toads a twist;
He's a beauty without paint O!

Henry Bennett
Every Day in the Year: A Poetical Epitome of the World's History,
  1902

The Well of the Book

When St. Patrick was one time amongst the Pagan Irish they
grew very fierce and seemed eager to kill him. Then his life being
in great danger, he kneeled down before them and prayed to God
for help and for the conversion of their souls. And the fervour of
the prayer was so great that as the saint rose up the mark of his
knees was left deep in the stone, and when the people saw the
miracle they believed.

Now when he came to the next village the people said if he
performed some wonder for them they also would believe and
pray to his God. So St. Patrick drew a great circle on the ground
and bade them stand outside it; and then he prayed, and lo! the
water rushed up from the earth, and a well pure and bright as
crystal filled the circle. And the people believed and were baptized.

The well can be seen to this day, and is called *Tober-na-Lauer*

(The Well of the Book), because St. Patrick placed his own prayer-book in the centre of the circle before the water rose.

Lady Wilde
Ancient Legends, Mystic Charms, and Superstitions of Ireland, 1887

Ruth Brandt

Three Irish Saints

In Downpatrick on the hill,
Saint Patrick, Bride, and Colm-Cille,
Underneath a leafy shade
In one grave at last were laid.
Saint Patrick guard us from all wrong
Let our faith in Christ be strong,
Saint Bride make clean our hearts and bless,
And fill them with thy holiness,
Saint Colm, comfort them that stray
And toil in exile far away
From everything that once was dear

In far-off places year by year,
For love of Ireland bless us still,
Saint Patrick, Bride, and Colm-Cille

John Irvine
A Treasury of Irish Saints, 1964

The Death of the Magician

And St. Patrick was called to the king outside the place where the fire had been kindled. And the magicians said to their people, 'Let us not rise up at the approach of this fellow; for whosoever rises up at the approach of this fellow will afterwards believe in him and worship him.'

At last St. Patrick rose; and when he saw their many chariots and horses, he came to them, singing with voice and heart, very appropriately, the following verse of the Psalmist:

> Some put their trust in chariots and some in horses;
> but we will walk in the name of the Lord our God.

They, however, did not rise at his approach. But only one, helped by the Lord, who willed not to obey the words of the magicians, rose up. This was Ercc the son of Daig [Daeg], whose relics are now venerated in the city called Slane. And Patrick blessed him; and he believed in the everlasting God.

And when they began to parley with one another, the second magician, named Lochru, was insolent in the Saint's presence, and had the audacity with swelling words to disparage the Catholic faith. As he uttered such things, St. Patrick regarded him with a stern glance, as Peter once looked on Simon; and powerfully, with a loud voice, he confidently addressed the Lord and said, 'O Lord, who canst do all things, and in whose power all things hold together, and who hast sent me hither, as for this impious man who blasphemes Thy name, let him now be taken up out of this and die speedily.'

And when he had thus spoken, the magician was caught up into the air, and then let fall from above, and, his skull striking on a rock, he was dashed to pieces and killed before their faces; and the heathen folk were dismayed.

Muirchú moccu Machtheni
St Patrick: His Writings and Life, 1920

St. Patrick and the Druid

The Apostle, wandering round Lough Monie's banks
In the clear sunshine of an autumn morn,
Came to a slope of sward whereon, o'ergrown
With lichen and with ivies garlanded
And orange-berried branches of the rose,
Gigantic columns rude, great plinths of rock,
In circle – a forlorn and desolate fane
Of that strange creed he came to overwhelm –
Stood lonely and silent. Part in awe he pored
Upon it, part in triumph, part remorse, –
As, on the morrow of some battle huge,
The victor gazes on the field of death
Strewn with the ruins of a nation's might
And glory, and remembers his own hands
Wrought the humiliation and the wreck.

Then from the shadows of a little grove
Hard by came moving slowly an aged man
Clad in worn raiment of a Druid priest,
And leaning on a staff; his long white hair
And snowy beard commingling almost hid

His shoulders and flowed downward to his waist;
But, under shaggy eyebrows, with the light
And vigour of youth, eyes of deep sapphire-blue,
Gentle but fervent, flashed. With grave salute
He hailed the Teacher, seeing in him his foe,
His vanquisher, yet seeming none the less
Contended in defeat.

       'All hail,' he cried,
'Great Victor, – if not wisest of the wise,
Least foolish of the fools that bask and flit
Their brief life out with dull or gaudy wing,
And go into the darkness whence they came
Knowing as much of that that is to be
As of the thing that was or that that is;
Or, haply, not least foolish of the fools
Neither, but only one that on the wheel
Is uppermost a moment, and the next
The lowest, even as I! – Welcome! … Let's sit
Here on this fallen stone, within the shade
Of this once mighty, now storm-wasted, oak,
And talk of things that seem not out of reach, –
Yesterday's battle of the violent septs,
Light gossip of the Lis, or – for to me
Such things are pleasant – beauty of the earth
And arching heaven, the golden autumn-leaf,
The white and wandering cloudlet high in air.'

And Patrick answered, 'Not of these. Of Him
Who made them.'
       And they sat.
              'Well, what thou wilt,'

The Druid said, and, smiling, laid a hand
Upon the Teacher's wrist: 'I know thee well, –

A man of strong belief and definite aim,
Incapable of doubt, – all fervour, thought,
Hope, love, hate, energy of body and will,
Working as one huge force to one clear end,
Never to be diverted until Death
All fervour, thought, hope, love, hate, energy
Of will and body crush to dust, for winds
To blow i' the eyes of men who have died not yet,
And vex and gall them. Such a man perforce
Bows with his own strong bent the baser mind,
Fills with his own strong faith the feebler heart,
Wields with his own strong will the weaker arm,
And may be, even as thou art doomed to be,
The slayer and supplanter of old gods.

George Francis Savage-Armstrong
Ballads of Down, 1901

How the Women Were Raised from Death

And wheresoever in his preaching went Patrick, the man of God, his lips diffused the healing knowledge, and the number of the believers was daily increased. And the Lord assisted his faithful servant with manifold miracles, and confirmed his doctrine, for that he falsified not the word of God, but always sought His praise and His glory. And on a certain day he came to a place called Fearta, where at the side of a hill two women who had deceased were buried. Then the man of God, approaching the grave, commanded the earth to be removed, and having invoked the name of Christ, he raised them up to life. And the women thus raised up, even in the presence of all around, proclaimed that their idols were vain, and that their gods were devils, Christ alone being the true

God; and in His name they besought to be baptized, and they attained their prayer. And the bystanders glorified God, and devoutly received his faith and baptism. Thus did the most holy prelate revive from double death the two women who were dead in the flesh; and their resurrection from bodily death gave unto many resurrection from the death of the soul.

Jocelin
Life and Acts of Saint Patrick
Translated by Edmund L. Swift
The Most Ancient Lives of Saint Patrick, 1874

St. Patrick and the Fairy

In the old books there are a great many stories told about meetings between the Saint and the Sidhe, meetings which were generally characterized by much kindly feeling and politeness on both sides. Here is one selected from many such.

Once when the Saint and his disciples were on the top of the famous haunted mountain Slieve Fuad, a very handsome youth, with long brown hair curling and dark eyebrows, and with a harp in his hand, was seen approaching.

'Who is the youth?' asked Patrick.

'His name is Cascorach,' replied a Gentile who was present. 'He is of the Tuatha De Danan and a good musician.'

The youth drew nigh and made genuflection to Patrick, who acknowledged that salute graciously.

'Prithee, O Cascorach,' said the Saint, 'give us now an example of thy art.'

'It shall be done, O Talkend,' he replied, 'and never before have I played for man or woman with so much pleasure as I shall for thee.'

Then he tuned his instrument and played. Never had the

Saint and his company heard before any secular music which was so ravishing.

'What do you desire in the way of recompense?' said the Saint.

'Heaven for myself,' said the Fairy, 'and good fortune for all who after me shall exercise this art.'

'It is granted,' replied Patrick, 'provided only those who profess music show no carelessness in their practice of the art.'

Then turning to one of his disciples named Brogan, he said, 'but for the fairy spell which infests it nothing could more nearly resemble Heaven's harmony.'

He also said, 'Banish not ministrelsy; at the same time I warn you not to be inordinately addicted to it.'

Anon.
All Ireland Review, 1901

Saint Patrick and the Serpents

There were serpents once in Ireland
Long centuries ago
In the meadows and the forests
Where men were loth to go.
By Saint Patrick they were banished
Beyond the Irish shore
And one was never seen again
From Slemish to Cahore.

John Irvine
A Treasury of Irish Saints, 1964

Ruth Brandt

St. Patrick and the Serpents

Second only to the shamrock tradition is the belief that St. Patrick drove the snakes out of Ireland. The common view is that all snakes and poisonous reptiles were expelled from Ireland by St. Patrick using his crozier after his period of fasting and penance for forty days on Croagh Patrick. Unfortunately we have again to admit that we are dealing with a tradition which has no sure historical foundation. The story is not found in any ancient Life of St. Patrick. Moreover it is discounted by the fact that Solinus the geographer, writing in the 1st century A.D., and treating of Ireland, mentions that there are no snakes there. Venerable Bede, writing in the 8th century, notices the same fact. Giraldus Cambrensis (1200) commenting on the absence of these poisonous reptiles says that certain people conjecture that St. Patrick and other saints of the country (*S. Patricium aliosque terrae sanctos*) drove them out. However, he considers it more probable that 'the soil had more to do with their absence than the faith'. Edmund Campion, in his Hist. of Ireland, cap. 2

(1571 AD) says: 'No venomous creeping beast is brought forth or nourished, nor can live here. Neither is this property to be ascribed to St. Patrick's blessing (as they commonly hold) but to the original blessing of God who gave such nature to the situation and soil from the beginning.' Moreover, as if to completely demolish the edifice of Patrician tradition, various other saints have been given this honour usually reserved to St. Patrick, notably Joseph of Arimathea, who, on the occasion of his alleged evangelising visit to Britain in the first century, is said to have visited Ireland also and expelled all poisonous reptiles from our shores. It must therefore be admitted that the evidence in favour of St. Patrick's expelling the snakes from Ireland is very slender: the story belongs to the class of myths and legends in general circulation during the Middle Ages and usually attached by some ingenious writer to a popular saint for his greater glorification. It seems thus to have been connected with St. Patrick.

Anon.
Down and Connor Historical Society's Journal, 1931

St. Patrick and the Snakes

The Season of Lent approaching, St. Patrick withdrew into a high Mountain on the western coast of *Connaught,* called *Cruachan-Aichle,* to be more at Leisure for Contemplation and Prayer. The Writers of his Life tell us, (and we leave the Relation to their Credit) that, in Imitation of our Saviour, *Moses,* and *Elias,* he here fasted forty Days, without taking any kind of Sustenance. *Joceline* goes further 'that to this Place he gathered together the several Tribes of Serpents and venomous Creatures, and drove them headlong into the Western Ocean; and that from hence hath proceeded that Exemption, which Ireland enjoys, from all poisonous Reptiles.' We seem to owe the Story of this Blessing, and considerable Priviledge, to this Monk of *Furnes*, a Writer of the 12th Century.

Sir James Ware
The Whole Works of Sir James Ware Concerning Ireland, Vol. 1
Revised and improved by Walter Harris, 1764

Saint Patrick and the Shamrock

Saint Patrick held the shamrock
Aloft for all to see
And said 'Behold this symbol
Of the Holy Trinity
Of Father, Son, and Holy Ghost,
One, yet one in three.'

John Irvine
A Treasury of Irish Saints, 1964

Ruth Brandt

St. Patrick and the Shamrock

Amongst all the traditions connected with St. Patrick there is perhaps none so widespread and persistent as that connected with the three-leaved shamrock. It is the popular belief that St. Patrick used the shamrock to illustrate the doctrine of the Blessed Trinity to the Irish people, and it is therefore with no little surprise, and even disappointment, that we discover there is no foundation whatever for this belief in any ancient life of St. Patrick.

The first definite association between our National Apostle and the shamrock is to be found in copper coins which were issued at Kilkenny in 1645 at the mint of the Papal Nuncio, Rinuccini. St. Patrick is represented with mitre and crozier and displaying a trefoil to the assembled people. The coins were popularly known as St. Patrick's money. Patrick Sarsfield similarly issued ½d and 1d. copper coins during the Siege of Limerick, 1690, figuring Erin seated holding a shamrock.

One of the first literary references to the wearing of shamrock is to be found in the Irish Hudibras written by James Farewell, 1689:

> Bring me a bunch of suggane ropes,
> Of shamrogs and potato tops
> To make a laurel.

He has also an allusion to Bryan Oge wearing on his head one shamroge. Ireland at the period was satirically called Shamrogshire.

Thomas Dinely, writing about the same time, gives us more picturesque detail. In his Journal he says (spelling modernised):

'The 17th Mar. yearly is St. Patrick's, an immovable feast, when the Irish of all stations and conditions wear crosses in their hats, some of pins, some of green ribbon, and the vulgar and superstitious even shamrocks, three-leaved grass which they likewise eat (they say) to cause a sweet breath. The common people and servants also demand their Patrick's groat from their masters, which they go expressly to town though half a dozen miles off, to spend – where sometimes it amounts to a piece of eight or a cobb apiece, and very few of the zealous are found sober at night.' A famous Oxford doctor maintained that the Irish owed their great energy and strength to their eating shamrock. Edmund Spenser mentions the same custom ...

The first literary reference to St. Patrick's connexion with the shamrock is to be found in a book written by Jacob Threlkeld, 1727, dealing with Irish plants. Laurence Sterne, writing in 1770, says: 'Patrick was canonized for illustrating the Trinity by the comparison of a shamrock.' And closely following on this in time is a picturesque account of St. Patrick and his missionary work from the pen of Edward Jones in his 'Musical and Poetical Relics of the Welsh Bards' (1794).

This story is approximately the popular tradition on the matter at the present day, but the identification of St. Patrick with the shamrock and the Trinity idea is not found before the Confederation coinage of 1645, nor is the literary account any earlier than 1727.

Anon.
Down and Connor Historical Society's Journal, 1931

The Queen, The Shamrock and St. Patrick
St. Patrick's Day 1900

This day is made memorable by the action of our Sovereign Lady the Queen. The skill of her Irish generals, and the valour unto death of her Irish soldiers, in South Africa, have saved – let the truth be told – the prestige of the Empire. And with a grace, queenly and womanly, the Sovereign has commanded all ranks in her Irish regiments to wear in future as a distinction, a sprig of Shamrock in their head-dress on St. Patrick's Day, to commemorate the gallantry of her Irish soldiers during the recent battles. Never had queen a happier inspiration; no, not 'in the spacious times of great Elizabeth'. I venture to say there is not an Irish heart worth having – and I think most of them are worth that – but is at the feet of the aged Queen Empress to-day, for this 17th day of March, 1900, is the first day of wearing of the green by royal command. What her ministers failed to find, her genius and her motherly heart found – in a moment, in a flash – a straight road to Ireland's heart. May no unwise hand shut it up in the years to come.

John Stephen Flynn
The Queen, The Shamrock and St. Patrick, 1900

St. Patrick's Black-thorn Flowers

Once on a day when St. Patrick came from Ireland on a visit to Auxerre, where he had studied with St. Germanus, on his way back to the island of his heart's love, he turned his steps southward to Marmoutier, the famous monastery near the old City of Tours where dwelt his friend and kinsman, Martin of Tours, the great saint and bishop …

And so, out through a bleak, bare, wintry world, a still, white world, that seemed to wear for its sins the sackcloth of a silent sorrow, did St. Patrick go by the little winding roads that led him southward along the banks of the darkly flowing Loire river.

With a cold azure sky above the bare branchy trees, from red dawn to white moonlight, he travelled on. By Anjou and Poitiers he went, and rested where the wintry night found him, now in the open plain, and now in the vast haunted stillness of some forest aisle where a blue curl of smoke on the air and a flush of scarlet from the open door of some charcoal burner's hut would give him welcome to the rest that was his for sweet charity's sake until the dawn of the white morrow's day …

And laying himself down there at the short, wintry day's end, in the gloom and silence of the narrow place, he would call on the strength of God to be with him, and the eye of God to watch over him, with the prayer that is called 'The Deer's Cry', the prayer that he had made in Erinn for his disciples, to enable them to overcome their enemies, and to pass safely, in spite of the enchantments of the Druids, on their way up to Tara on that fateful Easter Eve long ago …

And having prayed, rising up from that place, Patrick went out though the stillness of the starry night, away under the shadows of the dark fir trees, and over broad swathes of moonlight, until in the pearly coldness of the wintry dawn he found on his right hand and in a clear space, a great darkness of crowded waters that was the Loire river, where, all wide and free and shadowy, it ran eastward to the sea …

Cold and bitter cold the weather was, and around him where he lay the wintry storm hissed and raged. A black wind from the north came down, bringing blight and withering in its icy breath. But where the saint slept, under the black-thorn bush, in that hour, beside the dark Loire water, spring passed the way and it was April once again. The little shrub, spreading forth its branches, and shaking off the snow that rested on them, covered itself – as was its wont in the soft, rain-sweet Irish weather – with a wealth of blossom white as the snow flakes that fell around. In honour of the saint, and to remind him of the dear land to the westward, the land of Erinn, the little bush, in the depth of the wintry weather, had blown and blossomed by the river side there in the heart of the stranger's country.

On the banks of the Loire, on the slope of a hill, outside the little town of Saint Patrice, a few miles from the old City of Tours, this remarkable phenomenon is repeated year after year to this day. Amid the snows of winter the little black-thorn bush puts forth its flowers as in the Irish springtime. The tiny buds swell and the flowers expand, covering the branches with their wreaths of bloom, white as the snow that lies everywhere around. Year after year the unusual growth is repeated. No matter how severe the weather may be – such is the testimony of the old people of the place – the bush never fails to bloom at the same fixed period, in the depth of the winter season.

Cathal O'Byrne
The Irish Monthly, 1938

Saint Patrick's Day

A tiny sprig of shamrock from far across the seas,
Arrived for me this Patrick's day to wake my memories.
'Twas fresh and green and dainty not so very long ago,
Lying on the sweet brown earth in the land where shamrocks grow.

'Tis dying now, but though it droops, its magic lingers still,
To waft my thoughts across the seas to a cottage on a hill.
The half-door lies wide open, the turf fire's burning bright,
There's talk and laughter 'round the hearth – you see, 'tis
    Patrick's night.

But suddenly the laughter stills; a grey-haired woman speaks.
'I wonder now,' the old voice says, 'if, after all these weeks,
Tom's shamrock got to Canada as fresh as I would wish?
But sure 'twill freshen quickly in some water in a dish.'

A new voice calls a greeting old; a figure's at the door.
'God save all here,' he cries to them, as chairs scrape on the floor.
'God save you kindly!' answer they, 'come in an' welcome, Mick!'

'Tis 'Mick the Fiddler', old and grey, with fiddle and
   blackthorn stick.

The fiddle tuned, they take the floor; the 'Blackbird' gaily rings,
Then 'Good man, Pat!' and 'Swing her, Ned!' resound
   throughout the 'swings'.
The dancing ends, the fiddle rests; a colleen sings a song.
'Tis 'Danny Boy', and thoughts wing out on journeys sad
   and long.

The scene is changed. I roam again the haunts I used to know;
Where the snowdrops peep in springtime and bluebells used
   to grow.
There comes again the turf smoke's tang, scenting the evening air.
The moonlight gilds the mists that veil the bog that stretches
   there.

And once again I walk that bog, as memory turns its wheels.
And feel again the wind's soft touch, where the cutters load
   their creels.
I hear again the sleepy notes, as bird-folk close their eyes.
I see the lark in summertime go soaring to the skies,

To Ireland's Sons and Daughters each year the shamrock brings
Sweet memories of their homeland; of dear remembered things.
It brings us faith and courage; it seems to say 'Be true!'
We know we share our home-folk's thoughts, and share their
   prayers, too.

Patrick McDonagh
Shamrock Leaves: A Book of Verse, 1935

Birthday of St Patrick

On the eighth day of March it was, some people say
That Saint Patrick at midnight, he first saw the day
While others declare 'twas the ninth he was born
But 'twas all a mistake between midnight and morn

Mistakes will occur in a hurry and shock
While some blamed the baby and some blamed the clock
Till with all their cross questions, sure no one could know
If the clock was too fast or the child was too slow

Now the first faction fight in old Ireland, they say
It was all on account of Saint Patrick's birthday
Some fought for the eighth, for the ninth more would die
And who wouldn't see right, sure they blackened his eye

Till at last both the factions so positive grew
They each kept a birthday, so Pat then had two
Till Father Mulcahy, who showed them their sins
Said no one could have two birthdays, but twins

Says he, 'Boys, don't be fighting for eight or for nine
Don't be always dividing, sometimes combine
Combine eight with nine, seventeen is the mark
So let that be his birthday.' 'Amen,' says the clerk

If he wasn't a twin, sure our history will show
That at least he's worth any two saints that we know
Then we all got blind drunk, which completed our bliss
And we keep up the practice from that day to this

Samuel Lover, c. 1850

The Most Illustrious Order of St. Patrick

On the 5th February 1783, Letters Patent passed the Great Seal of Ireland, creating a new Order of Knighthood for that kingdom, the third of the three great national Orders, after the Garter of England, and the Thistle of Scotland. It was the first Order to be founded in the United Kingdom since the Order of the Bath more than half a century earlier. George III made his purpose for doing so quite clear: 'Whereas Our loving Subjects of Our Kingdom of Ireland have approved themselves steadily attached to Our Royal Person and Government, and affectionately disposed to maintain and promote the Welfare and Prosperity of the Whole Empire; And We being willing to confer upon Our Subjects of Our Said Kingdom a testimony of Our sincere love and affectionate regard, by creating an Order of Knighthood in Our Said Kingdom ... This is Our Royal Will and Pleasure and We do hereby Authorize and Require You upon Receipt hereof forthwith to cause Letters Patent to be passed Under the Great Seal ... for creating a Society or Brotherhood to be called Knights of the Most Illustrious Order of St. Patrick.'

Peter Galloway
The Most Illustrious Order: The Order of St. Patrick and its Knights, 1999

The Fundamental Laws, Statutes and Constitutions of the Ancient and Most Benevolent Order of the Friendly Brothers of Saint Patrick

The ancient and most benevolent *Order* of the *Friendly Brothers* consisteth of an unlimited number of Members, distinguished by the world *Friendly* inserted between their Christian and

Sirnames; who, in honour of *Ireland,* where this *Order* was first instituted, and hath long flourished, have put themselves under the patronage of *Saint Patrick,* and are therefore styled, *The Friendly Brothers of Saint Patrick.*

This Order is divided into two classes. One, comprehending all the Members of the Order, styled, *The Regular Friendly Brothers*; the other, consisting of such Regulars as, for their well-tried fidelity and friendship, have been initiated into the grand and solemn mysteries of the Order, and are styled *The approved and perfect Friendly Brothers;* who, from thenceforth, become Members of all Knots in the Universe.

The Assemblies of the Brethren are called *Knots;* signifying the indissoluble tie of love and friendship, wherewith they are mutually bound; and they are either Principal Knots, or Marching Knots, which all centre in the *General Grand Knot,* and *Select Grand Knot* ...

Every *Grand President* and *President* throughout the Universe, shall summon and convene his Knot on the Seventeenth day of *March,* annually, that being the anniversary festival of *Saint Patrick,* the Patron of the Order, except it shall happen on Sunday, when the meeting shall be convened for the following day; upon which occasion, all the Members shall appear in the ensign of the Order, being a golden Medal, on which shall be impressed *Saint Patrick's* cross, fixed in a heart, over which is a crown; the whole being set round with an emblematic Knot, embellished with trefoil, or shamrock leaves, and this motto, *Fidelis et Constans,* implying Fidelity and Constancy in Religion, Loyalty, and Friendship. On the reverse shall be impressed the Arms of the Order; namely, a Group of Hearts, in fesse, or, (as an emblem of the strict union of the Members of the Order) charged with a celestial crown of the same, in chief, in a field vert (the reward of their benevolence and fidelity;) round the shield, an endless Knot, set with shamrock leaves, mantling proper, and two emblematic dolphins, their faces downwards, argent; a label issuing from their mouths, with the motto *Quis Separabit*. This medal shall be worn pendant to a green ribbon. – And for the crest, on an helmet, and wreath of their colours, a wolf-dog, standing proper …

No person whosoever shall be admitted into this *Order* who does not profess himself a *Christian*. Nor shall any Religious, Political, National, or Party Debates, be permitted in any Knot. All profane *Cursing, Swearing,* and *Obscenity,* shall at all times, be avoided by the *Friendly Brothers*. And every Member who shall err herein in any Knot, or in the presence of a *Friendly Brother*, shall, for every Offence, pay Sixpence for the use of the poor, as a small memorial of his crime.

If any Member of this *Order* affirmeth anything upon the word of a *Friendly*, he is religiously to tell the truth.

If any Member of this *Order* findeth a continued *Friendly Brother* of the same in Distress, he is to afford him all lawful assistance, to the utmost of his abilities; and herein his own *Friendly* conscience is to judge how far he is to extend his Benevolence.

No *Friendly Brother* shall affront or quarrel with a continued Member of the *Order*. But, as the best of Mankind, in their unguarded moments, are subject to passions, if any Member of this *Order*, through the frailty of human nature should have the misfortune so far to forget the love he owes his brother, and the obedience due to these *Statues*, as to proceed to anger with a continued *Friendly Brother*, and disturb the peace and tranquillity of the *Order*, he shall not presume to decide his own quarrel according to the laws of pretended honour, by the barbarous practice of *Duelling*, unknown to the politest and bravest nations, but shall peaceably, and with due obedience, submit his differences to the decision of his Knot, who shall cause the offender to make sufficient and honorable atonement for his error. And the parties on both sides shall renew their Friendship, and in all points submit themselves to the friendly admonition and determination of their brethren, who shall judge on such occasions without prejudice or favour …

Finally, as the *Friendly Brothers* profess themselves to be lovers of all mankind, they shall therefore endeavour, by their advice and example, to promote and encourage among men the practice of all the social virtues; and to let their humanity, benevolence, and charity extend so universally to all that are distressed and miserable, as to render themselves, in the end, to be deservedly esteemed *Approved and Perfect Friendly Brothers* of the Ancient and most Benevolent Order of the *Friendly Brothers of St. Patrick.*

AGREED TO, IN A GENERAL GRAND KNOT, 17TH DEC. 1850, AND ORDERED TO BE PRINTED.

Sir John Kingston and Ralph Smith,
The Fundamental Laws, Statutes and Constitutions of the Ancient and Most Benevolent Order of the Friendly Brothers of Saint Patrick, 1851

The Celebration of the 17th March

The cult of St. Patrick was introduced to Continental countries by the very first missionaries from beyond the seas. His *natalis* on the 17th March, a birthday which remained, above all save one, sacred to every son of Erin, was celebrated as early as the seventh century at Luxeuil, at Peronne and at Fosses in Belgium; at Echternach, Corbie, Nivelles and Reichenau, probably from the very foundation of those abbeys. The celebration of the 17th March can be proved at Treves and at Landevennec, in Britanny, in the tenth and eleventh centuries ... many churches and monasteries boasted that they possessed some of his relics: St. Pierre of Rheims, Lisieux, Issoudun, Pfaffers in Switzerland, Lumiar, near Lisbon. The village of Neubronn (Wurtemberg) possesses a statue of the Saint which is greatly venerated throughout the district. In Upper Syria Patrick is invoked as protector of cattle; elsewhere prayer is said to him to obtain the cure of the deaf and dumb. According to a Breton saying, whoever kills an earwig with his finger gets the saint's blessing. This, no doubt, is attributable to the undying belief that the Apostle of Ireland drove out of that island snakes and all poisonous creatures. Irishmen held strange opinions about their saints. They had not the slightest hesitation in assigning to them the most extraordinary functions, and in conferring on them the very first places in the ranks of the Blessed. Thus the belief that St. Patrick would be called upon to judge all Irishmen at the last day, took firm root among them.

Louis Gougaud
Gaelic Pioneers of Christianity, 1923

Saint Patrick's Society of Montreal

On 17 March 1834, a meeting of Montreal's leading Irish citizens was convened at McCabe's Inn by Doctor Edmund Bailey O'Callaghan, a Montreal physician reform agitator, editor of the stridently pro-*patriote* newspaper *The Vindicator* and lieutenant of *patriote* leader Louis-Joseph Papineau. That evening, prominent reformers in the Irish community enjoyed a 'most excellent and abundant dinner' in the presence of O'Callaghan and the *patriote* deputy Auguste-Norbert Morin. A toast was proposed to 'Ireland as she ought to be – great, glorious and free', whereupon the assembled guests joined in singing 'Let Erin Remember the Days of Old'. Toasts followed, in succession, to 'The King', 'O'Connell and the Repeal of Union', 'Shiel, and the Patriotic Orator of Ireland', 'The Land We Live In', 'Papineau' (followed by a rendition of 'The Pilot That Weathered The Storm'), 'Union among the Irish and Canadians' and 'The Bishop and Clergy of the Catholic Church'. Respects were then paid to two prominent Irish Canadian reformers – Jocelyn Waller and Daniel Tracey – and tributes were proposed to 'Dr MacNevern and the Friends of Ireland' and 'Barrett and the liberal press all over the world'. The final toast at this all-male affair was offered to 'The Fair Sex'.

Nineteenth-century commemorative dinners were highly-ritualised affairs, and following the toasts, the assembled guests rose and proceeded to propose personal tributes to a wide variety of causes, including Papineau's Ninety-two Resolutions for political reform, The Irish Harp Society in Belfast, and even to O'Callaghan himself, with the newspaper editor and agitator Ludger Duvernay 'and the liberal press' who were expressing discontent with the political dispensation in the colony. This affair, held on the feast day of Ireland's patron saint, was a meeting of the *patriote* Irish, who were allied with several prominent French-Canadians in support of broader political and cultural projects in both Ireland and Lower Canada: Repeal of the Union and the advancement of Papineau's Ninety-two Resolutions. For men such as O'Callaghan, Repeal was paralleled by the *patriote* programme of political reform – both seen as struggles against inequities enshrined in the structures of British colonial government. But *patriote* sympathisers did not claim a monopoly on the politics of Irish Montreal – O'Callaghan notwithstanding, many of Montreal's leading Irish residents were of a more conservative stripe, and they placed themselves squarely in defence of civil order and the institutions of colonial government. These men assembled on Saint Patrick's Day the following year, at a dinner held at Patrick Sword's Hotel under the aegis of Michael O'Sullivan, later Chief Justice of Montreal.

In marked contrast to the previous year's dinner, the 1835 event boasted a guest list of the Irish community's Tories, including John Donnellan, who served as the first president of Montreal's fledgling Saint Patrick's Society. Toasts on this occasion were offered to the King, The Queen and the Royal Family, the Army, the Navy, 'Ireland, the land of our faiths. May unity exist among her songs of all classes and of all creeds,' and to Lord and Lady Aylmer, the colonial governor and his wife. This was the first official celebration of the feast of Ireland's patron saint held under the aegis of the new Saint Patrick's Society.

Kevin James
'Dynamics of Ethnic Associational Culture in a Nineteenth-
   Century City: Saint Patrick's Society of Montreal, 1834–56',
The Canadian Journal of Irish Studies, 2000

St Patrick's Day: Its Celebration in New York and Other American Places, 1737–1845

Boston

The earliest American celebration of St. Patrick's Day, of which record has been found, took pace in 1737. On March 17, that year, the Charitable Irish Society was organized in Boston, Mass., by a number of leading Irish Protestants. The Society is still in existence, though there is no longer any religious qualification for membership. The preamble adopted by the founders reads:

'Whereas; Several Gentlemen, Merchants and Others, of the Irish Nation residing in Boston in New England, from an Affectionate and Compassionate concern for their countrymen in these Parts, who may be reduced by Sickness, Shipwrack, Old age and other Infirmities and unforeseen Accidents, Have thought fit to form themselves into a Charitable Society, for the relief of such of their poor and indigent Countrymen, without any Design of not contributing towards the Provision of the Town Poor in general as usual.' …

Fort William Henry

On March 17, 1757, a celebration of St. Patrick's Day took place at Fort William Henry 'at that time the most northernly outpost of Great Britain in America'. It was located at the head of Lake George and had been built by Sir William Johnson, an Irishman by birth. At the time of which we write the garrison was largely Irish and included a battalion of Provincial Rangers under John Stark. Forty miles away was the French stronghold of Ticonderoga. On the evening of March 16, 1757, an extra ration of grog was distributed to the Irish troops in Fort William Henry, in which to 'drown the shamrock'.

Stark, fearing the effect on his Provincial Rangers, issued orders that no grog was to be given his command, on March 17th, except on a written order from himself. He then, it said, had it noised around that he could not fill out any orders as his right hand was lame so that he was unable to write. In the meantime, the French had made a forced march from Ticonderoga to attack Fort William Henry. On St. Patrick's night they fell upon the latter, perhaps thinking they would have an easy time of it.

They were repulsed, however, Stark and his Provincials taking a leading part in repelling the assault. Hon. John C. Linehan declares that 'The truth of the matter is, that with an Irish commander, Sir William Johnson, an Irish regiment in the fort, and a possibility of there being a part of the old Irish brigade in the French stronghold, St. Patrick had an all-around celebration and the attack was undoubtedly planned by the Irish exiles in the French service, who knew what the custom was on March 17, and thought to catch their Anglo-Irish opponents unawares.'

Fort Pitt

In 1763 a celebration took place at Fort Pitt (Pittsburgh). Capt. S. Ecuyer, in command at the Fort, wrote to Col. Boquet and in the course of his communication said: 'We had St. Patrick's fetes in every manner so that Croghan could not write by this express.'

Johnstown

In 1766 St. Patrick's lodge of Masons was instituted at Johnston, N.Y., being the first lodge organized, in that province, west of the Hudson river. It was still in existence at a recent period …

New York

St. Patrick's Day was celebrated in New York City as early as 1762. Of this fact we have a record. But the anniversary was, doubtless, observed here even at a much earlier period, if not by organizations, then by groups of congenial friends. We have seen that Irish residents of Boston celebrated St. Patrick's Day as far back as 1737, and, we have no doubt, the anniversary was as early recognized in New York.

Thomas Dongan, an Irish Roman Catholic, was made governor of the Province of New York in 1683 and held the office until 1688. There is little doubt that during this period the anniversary of St. Patrick was, in some manner, observed by the Governor and his friends and countrymen in these parts. It would be strange if this were not so, and we shall not be surprised if, one of these days, evidence, confirmatory of this, comes to light.

As a matter of established fact, however, we for the present date St. Patrick's Day celebrations in New York City from 1762. In the New York 'Mercury', under date of March 15, 1762, we find the following notice: 'The Anniversary Feast of St. Patrick is to be celebrated on Wednesday the 17th Instant, at the house of Mr. John Marshall, at Mount Pleasant, near the College; Gentlemen that please to attend will meet with the best Usage.' We find no further mention of the event but the same was, undoubtedly, a complete success.

A notable celebration took place in New York City in 1766. Some of the toasts offered on that occasion appear very strange in these days. It should be remembered, however, that British influences dominated the gathering and that if any of the assembled company disagreed with 'The Memory of King William', for instance, they very wisely kept their opinions to themselves. Some of the toasts, however, appear to have been quite commendable. The New York 'Gazette', March 20, 1766, and the New York 'Mercury', March 24, 1766, have the following account of the celebration:

> Monday last being the Day of St. Patrick, tutelar Saint of Ireland, was ushered in at the Dawn, with Fifes and Drums which produced a very agreeable Harmony before the Doors of many Gentlemen of that Nation, and others.
>
> Many of them assembled, and spent a joyous tho' orderly Evening, at the House of Mr. Bardin in this City, where the following Healths were drank, Viz.

1. The King and Royal House of Hanover.
2. The Governor and Council of the Province.
3. The glorious memory of King William, &c.
4. The Memory of the late Duke of Cumberland.
5. The Day; and Prosperity to Ireland.
6. Success to the Sons of Liberty in America, may they never want Money, Interest, nor Courage to Maintain their Just Rights.
7. Mr Pitt.
8. General Conway.
9. May the Enemies of America be branded with Infamy and Disdain.
10. May the honest Heart never know Distress.
11. The Protestant Interest.

12. May all Acts of Parliament, Contrary to the American Interest be laid aside.
13. Success to American Manufacturers.
14. May the true Sons of Liberty never want Roast Beef nor Claret.
15. More Friends and less need.
16. Conquest to the Lover and Honour to the Brave.
17. May we never want Courage when we come to the Trial.
18. The Lord Lieutenant of Ireland.
19. May the Enemies of Ireland never eat the Bread nor drink the Whisky of it, but be tormented with Itching without the benefit of Scratching.
20. *Our Noble Selves.*

Philadelphia

The Society of the Friendly Sons of St. Patrick, Philadelphia, Pa., was instituted on March 17, 1771. We may be sure that upon that occasion the memory of the Saint was duly honoured. Indeed, the date selected for organizing the Society, together with the name chosen, indicates the fealty of the founders to the great apostle of Ireland.

At the start, the Friendly Sons numbered 30 members, of whom six were classed as honorary. No creed lines were drawn, and in the Society 'Catholics, Presbyterians, Quakers and Episcopalians were united like a band of brothers'. The requisite for active membership was that 'the applicant must either have been a native of Ireland himself, or one of his parents must have been so, or he must have been a descendent of a member' …

Baltimore

Irishmen were among the first settlers of Baltimore. Fifty years before the American Revolution, Irish names are found on every page of the annals of the future Southern metropolis.

But it was not until after Independence had been achieved that the current of immigration from the Green Isle set so strongly toward Baltimore as to lead to special Hibernian observances and reunions in that city.

In 1791 the Irish Catholics were there in numbers large enough to cause the founding of St. Patrick's church, the second Catholic congregation in Baltimore.

Nurtured by Archbishop John Carroll, himself a Marylander of Irish blood, this parish steadily grew and for more than a century has been the chief centre of the religious observance of the day of Ireland's saint. Archbishop Carroll, until his death, took part annually, and the preachers and officiating clergymen included many who were, or later became, distinguished prelates of the American Catholic hierarchy.

Of the social and festive side of these recurrences a century ago less has been preserved, but many paragraphs are scattered through the files of old Baltimore newspapers. Every reader who has delved into a newspaper set of more than half a century ago must be painfully aware that more local news is omitted than is given. Nevertheless, we have gotten together a narrative which could easily be expanded beyond the limits of available space.

There are several curious points common to old Irish banquets. Probably the most surprising thing when comparing them to a modern banquet, is the large number of sentiments for which the guests were expected to raise their glasses; sometimes twenty, often thirty. Moreover, impromptu toasts were generally added.

Wheresoever men were fighting for independence – the Greeks in the Orient, the Spanish colonists in South America, the down-trodden masses of Europe – their deeds were not too far away to be applauded in Baltimore on St. Patrick's Day, at a time when the memory of Emmet and the chain of Irish revolutionists were also honoured. So, too, we find them declaring year after year against the political faction in America which favoured closer bonds with Great Britain which developed almost treasonable schemes when the war of 1812 came on ...

Charleston

The earliest celebrations of the day in Charleston, S.C., of which we have found mention, are thus set forth in the South Carolina 'Gazette and County Journal', Charleston, March 19, 1771: 'Sunday being St. Patrick's Day, the tutelar Saint of Ireland, the same was celebrated here yesterday by a number of Gentlemen who met on the occasion, and after partaking of a sumptuous dinner, spent the evening with that mirth and jollity, ever conspicuous to the natives of that Country.'

From the same paper, March 17, 1772: 'This being St. Patrick's Day, the tutelar Saint of Ireland, the same was ushered in by ringing of the Bells, etc.'

From the same paper, March 23, 1773: 'Wednesday last being St. Patrick's Day, the tutelar Saint of Ireland, the members of St. Patrick's Club, or Friendly Brothers of St. Patrick, celebrated their anniversary, when the following Gentlemen were elected officers of the said Society, viz: Hon. Thomas Knox Gordon, Esq., President; James Parsons, Esq., Vice President; Thomas Phepoe, Treasurer and Secretary; Edward Rutledge, Esq., and Mr. McCartan Campbell, Stewards.'

Can there, any further, be doubt of a St. Patrick's Society having existed in Charleston, S.C. in 1773, and perhaps previous to that year? We think not. Edward Rutledge was the brother of Governor John Rutledge, the dictator and military governor of South Carolina, both Irishmen. Edward Rutledge was a signer of the Declaration of Independence.

Savannah

St. Patrick's Day, 1812, was marked in Savannah, Ga., by the institution of the Hibernian Society of that city. The first president of the organization was John Cumming. The society fixed St. Patrick's Day as the occasion of its anniversary meeting and has ever faithfully observed the event with appropriate exercises. Possibly, during the Civil War, the celebration may, of necessity, have sometimes been omitted, but before the war and since the close thereof, the day has been duly observed. The preamble to the Society's constitution reads as follows:

> Irishmen, inclined, as they are by nature, to good-fellowship and charity, should not forget, in a foreign land, the duties they owe to themselves, their national character, and their distressed countrymen. These obligations are the more important to Irishmen because, during the long period of their oppression, Irishmen have been useful to themselves, their country, and their brethren, only in proportion to their exercise of those generous, charitable, and sterling traits with which it has pleased God to distinguish them among the people of the earth. Every motive, too, presses itself upon the heart of each true Irishman to foster an affectionate attachment for his native land – a country the more particularly unfortunate because her destiny has been unmerited, and therefore the more entitled to the tender consideration of her own sons, and of the good, the generous, and the enlightened of other nationalities.
>
> Driven from unhappy Erin by unrelenting tyranny, afflicted and persecuted Irishmen seek an asylum in this favoured republic, endeavouring to find, under the auspices of its liberal institutions, the only consolations that can remain to exiles thrust out of a beloved home by want and oppression. To these it becomes the duty of their more fortunate brethren settled in this free country, and enjoying the benefits of its hospitality, to reach out the hand of friendship, to tender the aid of a

delicate charity, and to offer any other assistance which fraternal, manly, and kindly feelings may inspire.

Impressed with these sentiments, the subscribers have agreed to associate themselves under the title of 'The Hibernian Society of the City of Savannah', and adopt the following constitution.

Section I, Article I, of the constitution declares that 'The Hibernian Society has, for its objects, the social harmony of its members; the maintenance of a filial attachment for the Mother Country; the aid of distressed Irishmen and their descendants; the relief of indigent widows and orphans of Irishmen and their descendants; the cultivation of good-fellowship, and the practice of charity.'

The constitution also declares that 'The Society is open for the admission of gentlemen of Irish birth, or, wholly or partly, of Irish descent, provided they have attained the age of twenty-one years,' and that 'No member shall be eligible to the office of President except an Irishman, or the son or grandson of a native of Ireland.'

Albany

In 1796, the Irish were sufficiently numerous in Albany, N.Y., to incorporate a church. St. Patrick's Day observances, in that place, may, therefore, be dated from about that time. In 1807, the legislature of the State of New York incorporated the 'St. Patrick's Society of the City of Albany,' and in 1833 the 'Hibernian Provident Society' of Albany was similarly recognized. Each of these organizations, no doubt, frequently observed St. Patrick's Day.

In 1810, St. Patrick's Society, just mentioned, had a celebration of the day, and another in 1811. The latter observance was 'attended by the governor, mayor of New York, Mr. Emmet and others,' and the following were among the toasts:

The Day and all who honor it – How long, O Erin, oppressed and degraded country, shall thy children bear the yoke? How long e'er their heartstrings vibrate to the music of thy bards, assembled around the festive board, commemorate the anniversary of our Apostle, unawed by tyrants, spies, or traitors?

The land we live in – Happy, happy land! here we can enjoy social mirth, here the hardy sons of industry meet their due reward; here no man is obliged to crouch to arrogance, intolerance or bigotry; exempted from the potent curse of tythe proctors, excisemen, reverend magistrates and military executioners, 'armed with a vigour beyond the law', we sit under our own vines and fig trees and bless the providence that led us to its peaceful shores.

The Land of Potatoes – May the characteristics of our country never be forgotten; earnest in love, war, hospitality and friendship.

Thomas Addis Emmet, Wm. James McNeven and their Compatriots – Who preferred incarceration to treachery, and who by their exertions have contributed to rescue the character of Irishmen from the calumny and obliquy of ignorance and bigotry.

Toast drank standing. The Irish Patriot's last speech – 'When my country takes her rank among the nations of the world, then, and not till then, let my epitaph be written.'

The Fair Sex.
Fair in face, fair in mind,
Full of grace and well inclined.

The Men who Fought, who Bled, who Died for the Country we now live in – for the principles we now cherish, and for the blessings we now enjoy.

The Sons of Erin, of Albany, N.Y., celebrated St. Patrick's Day 1812, in an appropriate manner and drank these toasts among others:

The memory of St. Patrick – May the divine precepts of the Gospel taught by the Irish Apostle, lead us to the felicity of a better world.

The State of New York – May its inhabitants enjoy all the felicity which their industry, their local situation and their patriotism deserve.

The American Flag – May its stars shed lustre on freemen, and its stripes chastise their enemies.

Our adopted country – its constitution and laws – may the wretch that would violate either meet his merited reward – the contempt of every honest man.

Washington

'A number of natives of Ireland and their American Friends' gathered around the festive board in Washington, DC, on St. Patrick's Day, 1812, and during the exercises duly honored the following sentiments from the toastmaster:

Erin – Sweet and fertile isle! Too long hath the divisions fostered by your enemies among your sons kept you in provincial thraldom.

Catholic Claims – The men who rise superior to religious disqualifications will soon burst the fetters of national subjection

Our adopted Country – divided it would fall a prey to the oppressors of our native land; united, it may bid defiance to a world in arms.

The Memory of our gallant Montgomery – Should it be necessary to march once more to Canada, his countrymen in America will be emulous to imitate his glorious example.

The Memory of Brian Boru – Who from the sands of Clonboy heroically drove the invading Danes into the ocean – Ireland has long sighed for such another exportation.

The peasantry of Ireland – brave but suffering people! Your wrongs will not always remain unredressed.

Robert Emmet – Ill fated in life but glorious in death; more virtuous men and better times will do justice to his character.

Arts and Manufacturers – May their progress in the United States, while they increase the resources of our industry, diminish those of our enemies.

The Harp of Erin – May its melodious strains have the same effect on the Orangemen of Ireland as they had on Thomas Moore, who from a Tory, has been transformed into a patriot.

The Fair Daughters of Erin and Columbia, lovely, loving and beloved.

Another celebration in Washington, D.C., 1812, was held under the auspices of the Society of the Sons of Erin, that city. Among the toasts were:

The Congress of '75 – its declaration to the people of Ireland that America should ever be an asylum to them from oppression, was worthy of the founders of liberty.

Irish Melodies – may their revival be the precursor of liberty to the country of their birth.

The Irish Harp – thy soul inspiring harmony shall yet celebrate the restoration of Irish freedom.

Irish Union – not that union which means subjection, but that which is formed by an oblivion of prejudices, an equality of rights and an amalgamation of interests.

American Manufactures – While their progress towards perfection tends to diminish British monopoly, it offers the best means of securing American independence.

Fredericksburg

The Hibernian Benevolent Society of Fredericksburg, Va., also celebrated St. Patrick's Day, 1812, in an appropriate manner. Among the toasts on that occasion we find:

The Day we Celebrate – and many happy returns of it to the sons and daughters of St. Patrick – may each return infuse new zeal for the benevolent cause that first made it a festival.

The Land we live in – perpetuity to its constitution and

government, and happiness to its people.

The Emigrant Sons of Erin – May they always be found foremost in the ranks in support of the government of this their adopted country.

The Fair – Nature's last, most perfect work.

The American Eagle – May her fostering wing be ever expanded to receive the oppressed sons and daughters of Erin, on their landing in this happy country.

John D. Crimmins
St. Patrick's Day: Its Celebration in New York and Other American Places, 1737–1845, 1902

The Hail of the Friendly Sons

Shall we who meet and part to night
Remember not our sires?
Shall we forget their age-long fight
Their quenchless battle-fires?
They handed us the freedom-flame
That spreads from sea to sea
They bade it burn in Ireland's name
Till land and race are free.
And we feel the thrill of their mighty hail
It comes with the boom of the guns
A heart and a hand for our fair land
The hail of the Friendly Sons.

J.L.C. Clarke, c.1771

Friendly Sons of St Patrick

ACKNOWLEDGEMENTS

I wish to thank the staff of the Linen Hall Library, Belfast, Libraries Northern Ireland, Down Museum and the Saint Patrick's Centre, Downpatrick, National Museums of Northern Ireland, the Hunt Museum, Limerick, Saint Patrick's College, Thurles, the Diocese of Cashel and Emly, and the Diocese of Down and Connor for their kindness and professionalism in answering my queries, and for their encouragement and support. I especially wish to thank my brother Paddy for responding so positively to my late-in-the-day (once, quite literally) requests for his photographic expertise.

The author and publisher gratefully acknowledge permission to include the following copyright material:

ANON., 'Veneration of St. Patrick in Italy and Spain', *Seanchas Ardmhacha* (1961/62) reproduced by kind permission of *Seanchas Ardmhacha*.

ANON., 'Crozier of Rev. Dr Slattery', library catalogue entry, in the care of the Archdiocese of Cashel & Emly.

BIELER, LUDWIG, translation of Muirchú moccu Machtheni's 'Death of the Magician', 'Patrick's Stay in Auxerre', 'The Birth of St Patrick and his Captivity in Ireland' from *The Patrician Texts in the Book of Armagh*. Edited with introduction, translation, and commentary by Ludwig Bieler (Dublin Institute for Advanced Studies, Dec. 1979) reproduced by kind permission of The School of Celtic Studies of the Dublin Institute for Advanced Studies.

BOURKE, CORMAC, 'Patrick' from McGuire, James and James Quinn (eds), *Dictionary of Irish Biography*, 9 Volume Set, © Royal Irish Academy 2009, published by Cambridge University Press. Reproduced by kind permission of Cambridge University Press and Cormac Bourke; 'Shrine of St Patrick's Hand', originally published in *Irish Arts Review* Vol.4 No.3 (1987). This version abstracted from the *Ulster Museum Gallery Guide* (1988), reproduced by kind permission of Cormac Bourke and the *Irish Arts Review*; 'What the Pilgrim Saw' from Turner, Brian S. (ed.), *Down Survey, 2000: The Yearbook of Down County Museum* (Down County Museum, 2000), reproduced by kind permission of Cormac Bourke.

BRADY, JOHN, 'A Mosaic of St. Patrick', *Furrow*, Vol. 1, No. 2 (March 1950) reprinted by kind permission of the *Furrow*.

CUMMINGS, D.M., 'Slemish', *Furrow*, Vol. 6, No. 3 (March 1955) reprinted by kind permission of the *Furrow*.

CURTAYNE, ALICE, *Irish Saints for Boys and Girls* (Helicon, 1955), copyright holder not traced.

DE PAOR, MÁIRE, 'The Cult of St. Patrick in the Vicinity of Drackenstein', *Seanchas Ardmhacha* (1961/62) reproduced by kind permission of *Seanchas Ardmhacha*.

DONNELLY, MAUREEN, *Saint Patrick and the Downpatrick Area* (1981) by kind permission of Maureen Donnelly.

GALLOWAY, PETER, *The Most Illustrious Order: The Order of St Patrick and its Knights* (Unicorn, 1999) reproduced by kind permission of The Revd Professor Peter Galloway.

HARBISON, PETER, *Irish High Crosses With the Figure Sculptures Explained* (Boyne Valley Honey Company, 1994) by kind permission of Peter Harbison.

HUGHES, KATHLEEN, 'Chapter IX: The Church in Irish Society 400–800' from O Crónín, Dáubhi (ed.), *New History of Ireland Vol. 1: Prehistoric and Early Ireland* (OUP, 2005) by permission of Oxford University Press; *The Church in Irish Society*, (ACLS History E-Book Project, 2008), in the public domain.

HUNT, JOHN, 'St Patrick in Art', *Furrow*, Vol. 4, No. 3 (March 1953) reprinted by kind permission of the *Furrow*.

HUNT MUSEUM, 'Silver reliquary bust HCM113' from www.huntmuseum.com/collection/silver-reliquary-bust, courtesy of the Hunt Museum.

IRVINE, JOHN, 'Three Irish Saints', 'Saint Patrick and the Serpents', 'Saint Patrick and the Shamrock', from *A Treasury of Irish Saints* (Dolmen Press, 1964), copyright holder not traced.

JAMES, KEVIN, 'Dynamics of Ethnic Associational Culture in a Nineteenth-century City: Saint Patrick's Society of Montreal, 1834-56' from the *Canadian Journal of Irish Studies* (2000), copyright holder not traced.

KAVANAGH, PATRICK. The lines from 'Lough Derg' are reprinted from *Collected Poems*, edited by Antoinette Quinn (Allen Lane, 2004), by kind permission of the Trustees of the Estate of the late Katherine B. Kavanagh, through the Jonathan Williams Literary Agency.

KINSELLA, THOMAS, *Faeth Fiadha: The Breastplate of Saint Patrick* (Dolmen Press, 1961), reproduced by kind permission of Thomas Kinsella.

LOSACK, MARCUS, *Rediscovering Patrick: A New Theory of Origins* (Columba Press, 2013), reproduced by kind permission of Marcus Losack.

LOUIS, RENÉ, 'St. Patrick's Sojourn in Auxerre', *Seanchas Ardmhacha* (1961/62) reproduced by kind permission of *Seanchas Ardmhacha*.

MAC PHILIBIN, LIAM (WILLIAM PHILBIN), *Mise Pádraig* (FÁS, 1961) reproduced by kind permission of Comhchoiste Timire-FÁS. Translation reproduced by kind permission of Mary Delargy.

MCGINNITY, GERARD, 'St Patrick's Church in Rouen', *Seanchas Ardmhacha* (1979) reproduced by kind permission of *Seanchas Ardmhacha*.

MCGRADY, FEARGAL PATRICK, *The Background and History of the Relic and Shrine of the Jaw-bone of Saint Patrick* (2010) reproduced by kind permission of Fr Feargal McGrady.

MESMER, GERTRUDE, 'The Cult of St. Patrick in the Vicinity of Drackenstein', *Seanchas Ardmhacha* (1961/62) reproduced by kind permission of *Seanchas Ardmhacha*.

O'BYRNE, CATHAL, *As I Roved Out: A Book of the North* (Blackstaff Press, 1982); *The Irish Monthly* (1938). Reprinted by kind permission of Roland Benner.

POCHIN MOULD, D.D.C., from *Ireland of the Saints* (Batsford, 1953), reproduced by kind permission of the Trustees of Muckross House (Killarney) CLG.

SCHOLES, WILLIAM, 'A Place Where Neighbour Reaches Out to Neighbour', *Irish News*, 13 February 2014. Reprinted by kind permission of William Scholes.

SIMMS, GEORGE OTTO, *Angels and Saints* (Four Courts Press, 1988) reproduced by kind permission of Four Courts Press, Ltd.

SLAVIN, MICHAEL, *The Ancient Books of Ireland* (Wolfhound Press, 2005) reproduced by kind permission of Michael Slavin.

WALLACE, MARTIN, *Saints of the Celtic Church* (Appletree Press 2008), reproduced by kind permission of Appletree Press.

WALLACE, PATRICK F., *A Guide to the National Museum of Ireland*, (Town House Dublin in association with the National Museum of Ireland, 2000), reproduced with the kind permission of the National Museum of Ireland.

WHISTLER, CATHERINE, 'Tiepolo's St Patrick Altarpiece', *Irish Arts Review* (1985) by kind permission of Catherine Whistler and the *Irish Arts Review*.

Images:

ALAMY, 'Saul Church, Downpatrick', AK1KAH, Design Pics Inc/ Alamy Stock Photo; 'St Patrick holding down a snake, 18th century engraving', EGW2T9, Pictorial Press Ltd / Alamy Stock Photo; 'Stained glass window, Saint Patrick, holding a shamrock and a staff', FNYK6E, David Clynch / Alamy Stock Photo; 'Statue of Saint Patrick at Lough Derg Pilgrimage Site, County Donegal', BBN48C, Radharc Images / Alamy Stock Photo; 'Struell Wells complex near Downpatrick, County Down', BF41HN, David Taylor Photography / Alamy Stock Photo; 'San Patrizio vescovo d'Irlanda 1746', by Tiepolo, Giovanni Battista (Giambattista), MP95B9, The Picture Art Collection/ Alamy Stock Photo; 'Slemish Mountain near Broughshane', E2D674, Hemis / Alamy Stock Photo'; 'St Patrick's Purgatory' by Claudius Joseph Ciappori-Puche (1822–87), and lithographer Franz Kellerhoven (1814–72), AY2T0D, Chronicle / Alamy Stock Photo.

ARCHDIOCESE OF CASHEL & EMLY, 'Crozier of Rev. Dr Slattery', permission granted by the Archdiocese of Cashel & Emly.

BRANDT, RUTH, 'Pascal Fire on Tara Hill', 'Three Saints', 'Patrick and the Serpents', and 'Patrick and the Shamrock' from Irvine, John *A Treasury of Irish Saints*, (Dolmen Press, 1964). Reproduced by kind permission of the Estate of Ruth Brandt.

BRIDGEMAN, 'St Patrick's Grave' (b/w photo), English photographer, (20th century) (after) / Private Collection / © Look and Learn / Illustrated Papers Collection / Bridgeman Images.

COGHLAN, EILEEN, 'Ethne and Fedelma' from Curtayne, Alice, *Irish Saints for Boys and Girls* (Helicon, 1955), copyright holder not traced.

DIOCESE OF DOWN AND CONNOR, 'St Patrick's Altarstone', Window: 'St Patrick arrives in Saul by boat', Window: 'St Patrick consecrated by Pope Celestine', from St Patrick's Church, Saul, reproduced by kind permission of the Diocese of Down and Connor. Photographs by Paddy Killen.

DIOCESE OF DOWN AND DROMORE, 'Window: St Patrick on Slemish', from Down Cathedral, Downpatrick, reproduced by kind permission of the Diocese of Down and Dromore. Photograph by Paddy Killen.

GAVIGAN, 'St Patrick lighting the fire at Slane', mosaic by Boris Anrep, Christ the King Cathedral, Mullingar. Photograph by Gavigan 01 at the English Wikipedia.

HUNT MUSEUM, 'Silver reliquary bust HCM113' from www.huntmuseum.com/collection/silver-reliquary-bust, courtesy of the Hunt Museum; 'St Patrick on the O'Dea Crozier'. The O'Dea Crozier is displayed in the Hunt Museum on behalf of the Diocese of Limerick.

NATIONAL MUSEUM IRELAND, 'Shrine of St Patrick's Tooth', 'Shrine of St Patrick's Bell', 'Bell of St Patrick'. These images are reproduced with the kind permission of the National Museum of Ireland.

NMNI, 'Shrine of St Patrick's Hand' from St Patrick's Church, Donegall Street, Belfast. © By permission of the Bishop of Down and Connor. Collection Ulster Museum.

NNP, 'St. Patrick Halfpenny', 'St. Patrick Farthing', reproduced by kind permission of the Eric P. Newman Numismatic Education Society.

PUBLIC RECORD OFFICE IRELAND, 'Jocelin's Life and Acts of St Patrick', 'Domnach Airgid' from Gilbert, John T. (ed.), *Facsimiles of National Manuscripts of Ireland* (Public Record Office of Ireland, 1874). Photograph by Paddy Killen.

SHUTTERSTOCK, 'Monument of Saint Patrick, Saul, Downpatrick', 13351651, stenic56 / Shutterstock.

TRINITY COLLEGE DUBLIN, 'Armagh Satchel', reproduced by kind permission of the Board of Trinity College Dublin.

INDEX

Page numbers in italics refer to illustrations